Quick guide

© Audit Commission 2003

First published in April 2003 by the Audit Commission ... ...tion and the National Health Service in England & Wales, 1 Vincent Square, London SW...

Printed in the UK for the Audit Commission by Holbrooks Printers, Portsmouth

ISBN 186240 459 3

Further copies of the handbook, and accompanying national report, and briefing are available from freephone 0800 502030

Index

 **Index**

Who the improvement handbook is for and how to use it

Who is it for?

The improvement handbook has been designed for managers and staff who work with disabled children and their families, across different agencies and disciplines.

Individual services and agencies can use it to improve their own services. But, the most effective way to use the change pack is for managers and professionals from different agencies and disciplines to use it to review and develop services together. Families told us that very often it was better co-ordination between different professionals and agencies that would make the biggest difference to the quality of their lives.

The disabled children study

This handbook is part of our disabled children study which also includes a national report and parent factsheets. It is based on research with over 240 participants, including:

- 133 disabled children and young people (7-19 years)
- 72 parents/carers (of children aged 0-19 years)
- 39 siblings (7-19 years)

and detailed interviews with over 60 service managers in five main localities in England and Wales, across a wide range of services and agencies, including:

- childcare and play
- social services
- youth services
- transport
- leisure services
- housing
- community and acute health services
- voluntary sector

Data returns on the type and level of services available in each of the five areas were also analysed as part of the work. The names of the children involved have been changed to protect identities.

How to use the handbook

The handbook is arranged in four themes:

1. Planning services to meet needs
2. The workforce
3. Children grow and move on
4. Inclusion in everyday life

Themes 1, 2 and 3 form the basis of all improvement work, regardless of the agency. Theme 4 looks at a variety of specific services in more detail. Each theme is split into a number of different sections, which can be read independently, or with other sections.

Each section is organised into six standard parts:

 Children and families talking

 Case studies

 Findings

 Signposting to other resources

 Key features of a good service

 Self-evaluation checklist

Our factsheets for parents and carers, which are being distributed via major national parent support groups are in appendix II. Factsheets are available on 11 different topics. Please copy them for parents you work with.

Our national report on services for disabled children and their families can be obtained from Audit Commission Publications on freephone 0800 502030 at £15, or, free of charge, from our website: www.audit-commission.gov.uk, where our other related reports can also be found.

1

Planning services to meet needs

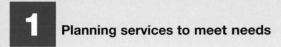

1.1 Understanding the local population and their needs

This section will be of interest to:
✓ managers and commissioners in all services and agencies, including voluntary sector partners.

See also: understanding local services and resources.

Families talking

If you fit a certain pigeon-hole you might be alright. If you've got autism, if you've got Down's Syndrome, they can place you. If you've got something like Clare's got, where does she fit in? And that's the biggest problem.

I kept bringing this up and 'Oh well, a lot of children do this' and 'A lot of children do that'. But when you've got one child who does all of them, then bells should start ringing. And 'Oh she's too young yet to be…' Any excuse not to spend money on assessment. We should have been listened to.

I know that I know what Craig needs. I'm not sure that other people know.

Services talking

They [families] want home support four days a week so they can get on with everyday life. We say we ask families what they want, but we still can't offer this to them.

There will be more and more profoundly ill children in the community. Some families will be able to cope incredibly with this, but needs will change...

Findings

The needs of disabled children, young people and their families are unique. They are often complex and change over time. The challenge is to understand these needs and develop a whole system of services around them – a system that is flexible enough to meet the requirements of individuals and diverse populations.

Many of the families we spoke to were in contact with a large number of public services on an almost daily basis. Other families received very little formal support. Despite these differences, disabled children, parents, carers and siblings all felt that appropriate, high-quality public services had an essential role to play in helping them to achieve a better quality of life.

But these families were frustrated and sometimes exhausted by dealing with public services. Their experiences sometimes led them to believe that local providers were more interested in slotting them into existing services, managing budgets and complying with procedures, than in meeting their needs. Many of the service providers we spoke to agreed that if families did not accept what was on offer, they risked being left without any support at all.

Families commonly encountered the following types of difficulties in accessing specialist services:

- unco-ordinated planning and provision, causing confusion and inconvenience;

- poor multi-agency working around transitions (for example, from children's to adult services, or from hospital to community services);

- eligibility criteria that were unclear, inconsistent between agencies, or so exclusive that families believed that they were intended to protect budgets rather than meet need; and

- high turnover in many staff groups (for example, learning support assistants, therapists, carers), leading to service gaps and poor continuity of care *[see section 2.2]*.

Disabled children and their families were often excluded from mainstream services, such as childcare, housing, leisure and transport, and had difficulties obtaining information about services that could meet their needs. Families then often had no choice but to chase from one service to another for support.

Many users had sympathy with overstretched staff working within limited budgets, and adjusted their expectations accordingly. But families were frustrated at perceived inequities in the way that services were allocated, observing that it was sometimes families who were most skilled, or most vocal, at articulating their needs who received support. Many parents told us that they felt penalised for 'coping' and believed services were waiting for them to break down, before offering support.

Service managers told us that the profile of needs among disabled children was changing rapidly, with an increase in the identification of autistic spectrum disorders, and in the number of babies born very prematurely and surviving with complex needs. They acknowledged the importance of multi-agency working to meet these needs, within a changing service context, where more services are being delivered in community and mainstream settings. Although these changes had important implications for the ways managers needed to plan and resource services, very few were able to quantify them and told us that this was an obstacle to developing needs-based services.

For all these reasons, a thorough understanding of local need is critical to providing user-focused, accountable and equitable services. For this to happen, the right information needs to be gathered and collated effectively, at a number of levels:

- the individual level, to deliver and monitor care that meets a person's specific needs and priorities;

- the operational level, for the day-to-day management and performance monitoring of services; and

- the strategic level, to plan and monitor services for whole groups and localities over time.

Localities with a good understanding of need

We found many services working towards assessments and care planning that truly involved users in defining their individual needs. Progress was aided by the development of joint assessment processes, and the government is leading the development of the Integrated Children's System (ICS) which offers a single approach to undertaking the key processes of assessment, planning, intervention and review. The National Service Framework for Children is to set national standards for disabled children's services for local implementation across health, social services and education *[see signposting]*.

At the operational level, localities working towards a good understanding of need were challenging protocols and procedures that obstructed the provision of needs-led services. For example, they were finding ways for staff in social services or education settings to support simple health interventions, rather than calling out a specialist nurse, the child's parents, or even taking the child to hospital.

One way to build a strategic understanding of local need is to maintain a register of disabled children, young people and their families. Since the Children Act 1989 local authorities have been required to establish and maintain a register of disabled children, and Quality Protects planning requirements have given this initiative further impetus. A number of successful registers contain just basic data, but some services are using the development of registers as an opportunity for understanding a much broader range of local needs in future. They are using locally specified information technology and involving partners from health, education and the local voluntary sector in pooling data about all their clients.

Localities can also use statistical estimates of prevalence rates for some conditions and needs in their population from government surveys. Other local planning documents can be helpful for profiling local needs, too, such as Joint Investment Plans and Early Years Childcare and Development Plans.

Another way to gain a 'snapshot' of clients currently known to services is to undertake a local census. On a 'representative' day – perhaps to coincide with relevant outpatient clinics, but not in the middle of school summer holidays – all caseload holders complete basic data returns about the clients seen. Using designated administrative support, this data can then be aggregated and used for planning purposes. This can be linked to the local census of children in need.

Finally, localities achieving a good understanding of local need are working to resolve a series of practical and 'cultural' issues, so that:

- users and other local people help to define their key needs;

- agencies work together and demonstrate ownership and support for a multi-agency register;

- agencies share relevant information, to understand the level of unidentified need;

- services/agencies have a shared working understanding of client confidentiality to facilitate information sharing;

- compatible information systems allow transfer of data between partners and minimise data input time;

- partners have shared working definitions of disability, agree how they record need and have transparent eligibility criteria; and

- partners agree clear accountability and resource for maintaining the register (in terms of database management, equipment and IT development).

Good practice

The Compass: Brighton and Hove's database of children with special needs

The Compass is the register of disabled children in the Brighton and Hove area. It is funded and supported by the city council and local health services, who have formed a strategic partnership for children with disabilities.

The Compass has been in operation for a year and a half, and is managed within aMAZE, a well-known local voluntary sector provider, offering advice and support for families. Registration on The Compass is entirely voluntary. Families submit their own details, defining a wide range of needs, such as the help that their child requires with mobility problems, challenging behaviour or toileting. Families are asked to indicate which services they are receiving, or need, from a range of statutory and voluntary services.

One advantage of placing The Compass' management and development within aMAZE is that families who register are immediately put in contact with a source of support and information. And there are other benefits to families of being on The Compass:

- disabled children are issued with a leisure pass entitling them to free access to swimming pools, with up to four siblings or friends; and

- parents and carers receive regular newsletters and handbooks that include information on local services.

By making entry onto the register voluntary and allowing families to define their own needs, The Compass is able to include a broad spectrum of families, including those who would not meet eligibility criteria for receiving social services.

An advantage for local partners, who have a shared responsibility and investment in the arrangement with aMAZE, is that The Compass is not led by a single agency, but is accountable and available to all of them. Partners promote The Compass to their staff and demonstrate how the register is of practical value for local strategic planning. For example, the co-ordinator provides regular profiles of registered families and recently used a search by council ward for families with children with Attention Deficit Disorder (ADD) and Attention Deficit Hyperactivity Disorder (ADHD) to advise on the best location for designated services for this group.

The Compass database, which cost several thousand pounds to develop, is still growing, with almost 600 families registered at present. The co-ordinator will use local census data to monitor growth of The Compass, and to identify areas where more promotion is needed, such as within local minority ethnic communities. The Compass co-ordinator currently spends 18 hours every week working on the register.

Critical success factors

- Committed local strategic partnership, with a clear, shared vision from the outset of the kind of information partners wanted on the register, and how it would be used.

- Parents needed a genuine incentive to register. Compass registrations have increased more than 50 percent since the introduction of the leisure pass 6 months ago

- A skilled, designated register co-ordinator whose priority is to maintain the register, and to act as an ambassador for it continually promoting its value to families and services.

For further information, please contact:

Jenny Broome-Smith
Tel: 01273 772289
Email: jenny@amazebrighton.org.uk

Support for parents of babies without a formal diagnosis:
The Children's Centre, Broxtowe and Hucknall PCT,
Nottinghamshire

A senior playworker recognised that parents of babies without a formal diagnosis sometimes lacked the right support from services. Further, she was aware that they often missed out on contact with other parents as a source of valuable information and support.

With permission from the Centre manager, the playworker started a small group session where parents could relax and talk in an informal and private setting, while their babies received gentle stimulation in a 'multi-sensory' room on site.

This small change had a big impact. Parents found the sessions a valuable opportunity to share their experiences and ideas with each other – often coming to terms with their concerns and finding emotional support for the first time, or perhaps just picking up 'regular' parenting tips about teething, feeding and other new experiences.

Through being empowered to meet unmet needs and deliver services in a new way, the playworker has also developed her skills and has had her client-centred approach reinforced.

Critical success factors

- Support from senior staff. The Children's Centre manager believes more junior staff should be encouraged to embrace new ways of working.

For further information, please contact:

Tracey Maycock (Senior Playworker)
The Children's Centre
City Hospital Campus
Hucknall Road
Nottingham
NG5 1PB
Tel: 0115 962 7658

Signposting

Council for Disabled Children, *Analysis of the Quality Protects 2002 Management Action Plans: Services for Disabled Children and their Families*, Council for Disabled Children, 2003.

Department of Health, *Integrated Children's System* (ICS) www.doh.gov.uk/integratedchildrenssystem

Department of Health, Department for Education and Employment, Home Office, *Framework for the Assessment of Children in Need and their Families*, Stationery Office, 2000.

Department of Health, *Data Protection Act 1998: Protection and Use of Patient Information (Circular: HSC 2000/009)*, Department of Health, 2000.

Department of Health, *Disabled Children Model (Numbers and Categories)*, www.doh.gov.uk/eor/children.htm, 1999.

D Gordon, R Parker, F Loughran and P Heslop, *Disabled Children in Britain: A Re-analysis of the OPCS Disability Survey*, The Stationery Office, 2000.

Council for Disabled Children, *Registering Effectiveness,* Council for Disabled Children. A review of the effectiveness of disabled children's registers, 2003.

Council for Disabled Children, *Dignity and Risk* (2003 forthcoming guidance including lifting and handling policies and practice.)

Department of Health, *National Service Framework for Children* (forthcoming).

Self-evaluation checklist

(This checklist is best used alongside the one in section 1.2)

How well do you understand individual needs?

Do you involve users in agreeing their own assessed needs, even if this requires extra help for the child or carer to express themselves? ■

Do you always prepare users for assessments, explaining what will happen in advance and giving them the option of inviting supporters or advocates? ■

Do you invite users to every meeting where you make decisions about their care – even if they only wish to stay for part of the meeting? ■

If you cannot do so, do you provide them with a copy of what was discussed and agreed in an appropriate format (for example, letter, phone call)? ■

Do you hold all your assessments in venues that are accessible for the user? ■

And if you have to ask the user to travel to an assessment or review, do you consider their transport, childcare and expense arrangements? ■

Do your operational policies and procedures help you to meet local needs?

Where possible, do you assess users' needs jointly with other professionals? ■

Do you share information with other agencies and professionals, where appropriate, to avoid distressing repetition and inconvenience for users? ■

Do key workers co-ordinate services for families, particularly for those with the most complex needs? ■

Do you use individual needs assessments to allocate workers to families and brief your staff, even if they are providing cover at short notice? ■

Do you regularly use needs data to profile caseloads, monitor activity and identify staff with difficult workloads who may need additional support? ■

Do you understand the specific cultural, religious and language needs of your users? ■

Do you use needs data to review your staff skills profile and to inform recruitment and training practice? ■

Do you have a strategic understanding of local needs?

Have you considered carrying out a regular profile of overall caseloads, to monitor trends in activity and changing needs? ■

Are you working towards sharing profiling information across local agencies and using it to inform joined-up, strategic planning? ■

Do you understand the full range and nature of people's support needs, including transport, housing, leisure, benefits and community safety? ■

And do you share this profile with mainstream services? ■

Do all key agencies in your locality (commissioners and providers, statutory and non-statutory partners) support a shared register of disabled children and young people? ■

If not, are agencies working towards this? ■

Is the information on the register analysed and used to build profiles of local needs and to inform service developments? ■

Does the register include information about profiles of disabled children receiving support outside your local area, so that you can review these arrangements and plan ahead to meet their needs more locally? ■

Does your register contain specific information, such as language needs, housing status or literacy needs, that enable you to engage with your users more effectively? ■

Have you considered using the register to match your workforce strategy to the needs of your users? ■

Are you aware of individuals and groups who do not use your services? ■

Do you understand the implications for these families? ■

Do you understand the implications for planning and delivering your services? ■

Have you considered the 'whole systems' implications of this for other specialist and mainstream services? ■

Are you working with other agencies towards implementing the National Service Framework for Children? ■

1.2 Understanding local services and resources

This section will be of interest to:
✓   managers and commissioners in all services and agencies, including voluntary sector partners.

See also: understanding the local population and their needs.

Families talking

It's not what you're entitled to, it's what's available.

Once you get a service it's usually quite good, but the problem is getting it. The first problem is knowing about it. The second problem is persuading somebody that you need it. And then the third problem is finding someone who can deliver it...

I said I want someone to wash the floors, wash the windows, wash the door handles, wipe the skirting boards. 'We don't do that sort of thing – we only do dusting and hoovering. And I said I haven't got any carpets and dusting isn't a priority. And I think there was a genuine feeling of frustration on social services because they couldn't do anything.

Services talking

We have to look at how to get the service out to people. We currently offer a service to those who can get here.

At present, we can't even signpost to other services, as we don't know about other services and resources elsewhere. [occupational therapist working in a housing department]

We don't have a clear enough picture. We expect communities to know about services, but they don't necessarily.

We assume we're alright, but I think families find our services really confusing.

Findings

Users told us about some excellent local services. Here families were clear that the right resources delivered by the right people at the right time – with users helping to define what is 'right' – really improved their quality of life.

But, sadly, much more often, families experienced services that:

- felt fragmented or unco-ordinated;

- were inflexible and centred on operational constraints, rather than individual needs;

- gave out limited or poor information; and

- excluded people from support because of their individual needs, age or where they lived.

Service stakeholders recognised and often shared users' frustrations with fragmented services. They acknowledged that services had often developed in isolation, without shared accountability, and with different priorities and funding streams, and were often planned without an overview of the 'whole system'. This could lead to inefficient use of resources through gaps and duplications in services. A frequent example was the parallel provision of health and social services residential short-break schemes, rather than a more diverse range of provision across the two services, including more home and community-based options. Lack of strategic planning in the play and youth sectors also led to gaps: in the range of activities offered, in services for children of certain ages, and in services for children with particular needs. In more rural areas, with poorer transport links, the resulting lack of suitable local services was particularly distressing to families.

Services were also struggling to join up at the operational level, with users' needs often frustrated by the different protocols and constraints that applied to different services, such as specialist transport that would collect a disabled child from school and take her home, but would not take her from school to her foster family for short breaks. Or policies that would not allow her to take her electronic communication aid with her from school to her short-break centre. Differences in age-related eligibility criteria between services created other gaps that left users without services at critical times.

Mainstream services often failed to consider disabled children, young people and their families. For example, many disabled children and their families said they could not use a local swimming pool because of a lack of suitable changing facilities. Parks often did not provide gates, paths and play equipment that were accessible for disabled children and young people. And many disabled pupils in mainstream schools found that they were still excluded from some lessons and activities, because of inaccessible classrooms, or because teachers were unable or unwilling to include them in PE lessons or school trips.

Accurate service information is critical to enable parents and children to navigate the current maze of fragmented services. We found that families often had to rely on other families, support groups, or a particularly helpful member of staff, to find out about basic services. Families without this sort of advice sometimes heard about services too late, or had gone without support for years.

Staff were willing to challenge traditional patterns of services and working practices, to better meet users' needs. In one area, which had historically provided services almost exclusively for children with learning disabilities, staff were beginning to develop services for other disabled children. Many localities were also striving to remove gaps and discontinuities in services by improving multi-agency working (for example, at transition). And in many areas services were starting to respond to the Disability Discrimination Act 1995 and the SEN and Disability Act 2001, by making their mainstream services more inclusive.

Statutory flexibilities, such as pooled budgets and the joint employment of staff, offer promising opportunities for a 'whole systems' approach to services although uptake has so far been slow *[see section 1.3]*. New governance structures, like Children's Trusts, also offer opportunities for services to work together in a more co-ordinated way. But for any of these new initiatives to make a difference, planning processes need to be informed by a detailed understanding of local needs and a systematic and comprehensive review of current activity. Some services we reviewed had started by auditing what was 'on the ground' before considering structural change. Meaningful user involvement is also an integral part of any successful change programme, because families need to be able trust that the services they have come to depend on will not be withdrawn before others are established *[see section 1.4]*.

The National Service Framework for Children is to set national standards for disabled children's services for local implementation across health, social services and education.

Localities that are working to understand their services and resources

Start by:

- engaging stakeholders in all agencies, at all levels: users, frontline, managerial and strategic level staff;

- sharing information between agencies and developing shared working definitions of need and disability *[see section 1.3]*; and

- mapping user needs *[see section 1.1]*.

Next they draw up:

- a multi-agency map of specialist services for disabled children, young people and their families;

- a map of the 'everyday life' mainstream services, such as housing, leisure and transport; and

- look at how services are provided: funding streams, hours available, eligibility criteria, co-terminosity, age cut-offs, locations, accessibility of venues, and so on.

Finally they:

- identify and challenge gaps and duplications in the whole system;

- identify opportunities to provide services in a more user-focused, effective and efficient manner, such as pooling budgets, joint commissioning, forming multi-disciplinary teams, and sharing accessible venues; and

- with this level of understanding, start to re-design services to meet identified needs.

 ## Good practice

Carmarthenshire: service allocation meeting (SAM) to streamline local services

By auditing local services, managers in Carmarthenshire found out that over 30 related services operated across the County, providing support in people's homes and the community. They realised that statutory services often duplicated roles and resources with the voluntary sector.

Clients were often referred to more than one service, in the belief this would speed up the time it took to deliver support. All of this activity took its toll. In 2002, for example, it was taking over six weeks for some families to receive support from the Family Aide Service, from time of referral to the introductory meeting with the family. Services and users agreed that these delays were unacceptable and SAM was piloted.

SAM is a county-wide allocation and response system that looks at all new referrals to disabled children's social services which meet the eligibility criteria. SAM involves all local stakeholders in the social care sector, and meets twice a month.

There is close liaison with health and education services, to facilitate onward referrals to these services.

More streamlined and organised referrals have meant that waits for support across a range of agencies have fallen dramatically. Families now wait 14 days from referral to introductory contact. This target is met in up to 90 per cent of cases, and SAM partners are working to reduce waits further.

Over time, SAM aims to rationalise the range of services and providers offering support. They hope that from a clear 'menu' of local services, SAM will enable services to allocate staff with the best fit of skills to match client need.

Establishing SAM with involvement from all stakeholders has also led to more open relationships between the statutory and voluntary sectors, providing an opportunity for joint working to improve the quality and consistency of practice.

Stakeholders are now evaluating and monitoring the impact of these changes on the wider service system and on individual families.

Critical success factors

- Multi-agency involvement: senior staff from partner agencies gave time and commitment to the process.

- Ownership of the new system by frontline staff: frontline staff developed the new operational protocol for the Family Aide Service and piloted it.

For further information, please contact:

Marya Shamte (Service Manager)
Tel: 01554 745 150

Planning services to meet needs

1.2 Understanding local services and resources

 Signposting

British Association for Community Child Health – Child Development and Disability Group, *Standards for Child Development Services: A Guide for Commissioners and Providers*, 2000.

Department of Health, *National Service Framework for Children*, (forthcoming).

Self-evaluation checklist

[This checklist is best used alongside the one in section 1.1]

Specialist services

Are all key agencies in your locality – commissioners and providers, statutory and non-statutory partners – working towards mapping local needs and services for disabled children, young people and their families? ■

> *Is the mapping designed to help agencies to identify unmet needs and possible duplication of services?* ■

Have you considered how disabled children and young people, and their families, can be encouraged and supported to participate in needs and service mapping? ■

Will your local service map pay attention to the needs of people:

> *– from black and minority ethnic communities?* ■

> *– from rural and dispersed communities?* ■

Do all key agencies in your locality have explicit and well-understood eligibility criteria for their services? ■

Can all key agencies in your locality clearly identify their current expenditure on disabled children's services, and their sources of funding? ■

> *Have you identified the resources potentially available for this client group?* ■

Will your locality mapping feed into a comprehensive, up-to-date and accessible directory of services for users? ■

Mainstream services

Does local planning for mainstream or non-specialist services explicitly address the inclusion of disabled children and young people? ■

Do mainstream service representatives participate in specialist planning for disabled children, young people and their families? ■

Have specialist services identified how they can participate in mainstream planning? (for example, by agreeing who will go along to mainstream planning processes and forums) ■

Do you aim to ensure that all local policy, from community safety, to urban planning, to economic regeneration addresses the needs of:

children and young people in general? ■

disabled children? ■

Findings

Unsurprisingly, we found that better joined-up care would substantially improve families' experiences of services.

Families – particularly those with the most complex and diverse needs – were dependent on a disjointed network of agencies and professionals, which resulted in multiple contacts with different staff and repetition of information. They wanted co-ordinated care that felt 'seamless'. Most staff we spoke to acknowledged this, and wanted to work with each other to improve experiences and outcomes for users. They also recognised that joined-up working could deliver more consistent standards and better use of scarce resources.

Agencies highlighted their legacy of separate development and funding as obstacles to joint working. Different geographical boundaries compounded the issues. Some staff acknowledged lack of clarity about one another's roles, or professional standards. But despite very complex service configurations, a tangle of children's policy and planning routes, and cultural challenges to partnership working, we were able to identify progress in some areas.

Some users did experience joined-up care. In some localities, services were pulling together and nominating a single key worker to be their point of contact for families. The key worker's role was not to deliver all the services, but to co-ordinate them and to provide continuity and advice for families. Our research showed that these schemes were highly valued by families. However, key working projects were often small-scale, focused on clients with the most complex needs, and had time-limited resources. Many families who did not fall within local schemes, but knew about them, wished they could be extended.

Joint referral and allocation processes also allowed services to pull together. Here, referrals were brought back to a panel or team. The team might be fully integrated, based together, share management and be jointly employed by local agencies, or could be a 'virtual' team based in separate agencies who came together for this work. The team agreed which professional was best placed to make a single initial assessment. It was shared with other professionals, and a joint decision about longer-term work was then made, ideally at a meeting involving the family. Some panels had a pooled budget for services such as short breaks which they felt led to a more transparent system for families and referrers, and provided the panel with a better overview and control of local resources.

But in many other instances, families remained confused and frustrated by services that did not work together, for example, short-break schemes that could not cater for children who needed basic clinical interventions *[see section 2.1]*.

To address these problems, services need to engage in change at a strategic level; and there is some evidence of progress towards this in some areas. We have seen multi-agency forums and strategic planning groups emerging, pulling decision makers together around disabled children. Those involved in successful forums stressed the importance of real 'buy-in' and commitment from partners. Diverse membership, with user, voluntary sector and mainstream service representation (for example, housing and leisure) further strengthened the capacity of groups to build relationships for future planning.

The most advanced forums were beginning to view needs and resources in the locality as part of a whole system and were, for example, developing joint registers. Others were working together to fund joint posts, or create teams for 'cross-cutting' needs, like behaviour support. Some were going much further and committing to structural and financial integration by forming Pathfinder Children's Trusts. The National Service Framework for Children is likely to set national standards for joint working across a range of agencies, in particular health, social services and education.

Features of good joint working

At a strategic level, agencies committed to better joint working are:

- forming strategic multi-agency planning forums;

- using flexibilities to pool budgets and jointly appoint staff;

- exploring the potential of new structures such as Children's Trusts; and

- involving disabled children and their families in developments.

But successful partnerships are aware that structural change is not sufficient for step change in service delivery. Improved services will only follow if senior level stakeholders show a practical commitment towards joint working, by being prepared to change organisational attitudes and day-to-day processes.

At operational level, plans to improve inter-agency and inter-disciplinary working are likely to include joined-up:

- referrals;

- assessments; and

- client allocations.

To achieve this, managers and professionals will be working together to find ways of overcoming historically incompatible:

- definitions of need;

- information systems; and

- working practices.

At the individual user level, we have seen the very beneficial impact of key working for a limited number of families. Progress now depends on rolling out the lessons that these initiatives teach us, so that every user receives a service that feels integrated and seamless.

Good practice

Fusion-4: Integrated services around the child

Fusion-4 is a new service for disabled children, young people and their families in the Mansfield area. It was developed in response to families' experiences of fragmented and confusing services, which was resulting in them having to repeat their stories to a myriad of professionals, and having no clear focus for information or support.

Fusion-4's board members are senior managers in the voluntary sector, health, education, social services, Connexions, youth, community and play services.

The key project objectives are:

- to be driven by the needs of service users, with strong user involvement in project developments and processes;

- to be a single local access point for services;

- to provide multi-agency team assessments and services at an early stage of need; and

- to develop co-ordinated services that are jointly commissioned and provided.

A multi-agency assessment identifies key issues and concerns for the child and family. It describes a baseline for service need and is the information source for all agencies involved in care. The child is helped to contribute through the 'ME!' booklet, which helps them to describe their preferences, ways of communicating, needs and wishes. These assessments are fed into a multi-agency action planning meeting.

Fusion-4 is still developing, but a small core, multi-agency team will carry a caseload of families. From here, keyworkers will support families and help to co-ordinate appropriate services, using joint tools and protocols. The team will form a network around the child, improving information sharing and providing more joined-up care delivery.

Critical success factors

- By using task groups to develop ideas and new ways of working, Fusion-4 have found that they can involve everyone and keep people on board. While the service is undergoing big changes, and resolving uncertainties, task group members can see results and the role gives them something 'bite sized' to focus on. Task groups can also be used to 'thrash through' contentious issues without holding up the wider decision making process.

- By using a variety of approaches Fusion-4 has enabled disabled children and young people to make their views heard effectively.

- Fusion-4 have learnt that it is critical to ensure that representatives from partner agencies really are feeding things back to the right people at the right level in their own organisations and putting agreements into action. Partners may sign up to implementation, but it is worth checking that they are really making things happen in their own organisations.

For further information, please contact:

Lesley Phair (project manager)
Tel: 01623 414 114 x 4575
Web: www.fusion-4.org.uk

See also:

Section 2.2 Fusion-4 case study on involving users in recruitment.
Section 3.1 Good practice case study on keyworking.

Signposting

G Limbrick-Spencer, *The Keyworker*, Wordworks, 2001.

Care Co-ordination Network UK,
www.york.ac.uk/inst/spru/ccnuk.htm, Tel: 01904 433605

Medway Positive Parenting Network, www.medwayppn.org.uk, an award-winning internet based multi-agency information service for parents

Department of Health, *National Service Framework for Children*, (forthcoming)

Self-evaluation checklist

At the individual level

Is there a single, comprehensive source of information about local services for families? ■

Are you involving users in evaluating your services, to identify the gaps between services and how users would like to see these change? ■

Do you allocate key workers to families with the most complex needs? ■

At the operational level

Have you considered a single route for referrals into related services? ■

Do services around disabled children share a single initial assessment and allocation process? ■

Are you working towards this? ■

Do you have an agreed joint policy on information sharing with other agencies, including data confidentiality? ■

Are you exploring and using the full range of policy flexibilities that can facilitate joined-up working? ■

Do you jointly advertise, recruit and fund staff in key positions? ■

Have you considered the value of a joint panel for managing short-break services? ■

Have you considered a joint equipment store or a pooled budget for some equipment? ■

Are you working with other agencies towards implementation of the National Service Framework for Children? ■

At the strategic level

Are you forming a multi-agency forum as the focus for planning services for disabled children? ■

Are you involving the voluntary sector and key mainstream services? ■

Have you considered establishing a joint register? ■

And a joint service and resource map? ■

Young people talking

He just draws Xs on my foot, he doesn't even speak to me, he's just interested in my feet.

I can't go on any of the rides. If they could get rid of the embankment thing because they don't really need it... Places like the park and that, they need to make it better for disabled children because there's not much activity around here for disabled children.

Families talking

What you need is views of parents to inform staff.

When she was first diagnosed they used to speak in all this technical stuff that I couldn't understand and it got to the point one day when I said 'Excuse me, I am in the room and I'd like to know what you are talking about' and since then things have been much better. Because otherwise they do talk over your head.

Professionals think they know better. 'I can handle this situation, we're dealing with children like this all day long'.

If you pass an opinion there and it goes against the grain then it's not 'Why do you think that? Why do you feel that?' It's 'Oh right'......You've gone against what they've been discussing.

'We can't do anything about that, it's not our fault, we don't know anything...' Why are you answering the phone if you don't know anything? You phone wheelchair services, it's a prime example, unless you actually get to speak to the people who deal with the wheelchairs, the people who answer the phones they can't give you any [information].

Findings

The best way to make sure that services meet needs is to ask the people who use them for their views, experiences and preferences. Our study identified a number of issues for families with communicating their needs to professionals and service providers, both in everyday communication and in getting the opportunity to influence the way that services are provided.

Young disabled people taking part in our study frequently commented that some professionals did not speak to them at all. Instead they spoke to their parents, as if the young person was not in the room. However, parents also noticed a tendency for professionals to talk to each other, or use language that they could not understand. They often felt their own knowledge and expertise in caring for their child and knowing his or her needs was being overlooked in favour of fixed professional views and procedures.

On a broader level, some families commented that parents could improve services if they were given the opportunity to have input into how they were managed and delivered. Few of the people we spoke to mentioned being consulted about services or offered an opportunity to contribute their views, although our research with local service providers did indicate that a number of small-scale consultation initiatives were being undertaken. Increasingly, services are recognising the need to consult more with this client group, but at present good practice is limited.

The importance of consultation and the involvement of service users is emphasised in legislation and guidance such as:

- comprehensive performance assessment, which makes consultation of service users essential to local authorities' performance rating;

- Health and Social Care Act 2001 and Healthcare Professions Act 2002, which provide for greater involvement of patients in decision making;

- the Children Act 1989, which states that children should have a say in decisions that affect them;

- the Human Rights Act 1998 and UN Convention on the Rights of the Child, which both emphasise the right to communication and self-expression; and

- Framework for the Assessment of Children in Need and their Families, which gives guidance on involving disabled children *[see signposting]*.

There are now many innovative approaches to consulting young disabled people and their families. Initiatives such as the 'Ask Us' projects have demonstrated ways to involve young people with a range of impairments in improving services. These creative projects gave young disabled people the opportunity to evaluate local services, to test how disabled-friendly they were, and to report back to service providers *[see signposting]*.

Disabled young people such as those who are involved in the Triangle consultative group and the Manchester Young Disabled People's Forum *[see case study below]* have also led the way in developing research and consultation techniques. They have actively disseminated resources, including training videos and handbooks, to help service providers learn about their views and experiences *[see signposting]*, as well as offering consultancy services. Specialist consultancies are able to conduct sensitive research with children with the most complex communication needs, or to train staff to do so themselves.

Increasingly, user representation is provided on management committees of individual services, and multi-agency forums, but usually involving parents rather than young people themselves.

Good practice

Young Disabled People's Project Greater Manchester

The Young Disabled People's Project has been developed within the Greater Manchester Coalition for Disabled People (GMCDP) over the last 13 years. It came into being when it was identified that local services such as youth clubs did not include disabled young people.

GMCDP gained funding to provide two ten-week Independent Living Courses and attracted many young disabled people throughout the ten boroughs of Greater Manchester. Through this the Forum emerged and now 40 young disabled people are active in the project. Service providers, parents of young disabled people and young disabled people themselves contact the Forum on a regular basis for support and information, on issues such as independent living, sexual health, housing and employment. The Forum is funded jointly by the local authority and health authority.

Forum members attend group meetings every three weeks, and training courses run within the Forum. They receive around 200 – 250 contacts a year from or on behalf of other young disabled people seeking support and information. The Forum has an 'open door' policy throughout the week. They also have five young disabled voluntary workers, and a drama group with 15 members who travel around the UK using drama to highlight the barriers that young disabled people face and how to overcome them.

Local authorities, service providers and study groups contact the Forum for consultation. Often members join steering groups, where they take part in decision-making and influence how local services are run.

The Forum's achievements include:

• Producing positive image posters.

- Producing a short amateur video around positive images.

- Involvement in planning the 'There 4 Me' website with the NSPCC.

- Producing the CD ROM 'Our Life Our Say' *[see Signposting]*.

- Founding the campaigning group 'Barrier Free Zone'.

- Gaining funding for a peer support/outreach project.

The Forum has been highly successful in providing consultation, gaining funding, becoming involved in decision making and bringing about change. The young people taking part have also benefited – taking control of their lives, gaining confidence and skills.

Critical success factors

- The Forum is part of an organisation managed and staffed by disabled people. The environment is accessible and non-discriminatory.

- All individual access needs are met so no-one is prevented from taking part.

- Young people have ownership of the group and know that they are being listened to.

- Forum members have seen their consultation work affecting decisions and bringing about change.

- Young disabled people set the agenda when approached for consultations.

For further information, please contact:

Audrey Stanton
Project Worker GMCDP's Young Disabled Peoples Forum
Tel: 0161 273 8141
Email: gmcdpydpf1@btopenworld.com

Signposting

Audit Commission, *Connecting with Users and Citizens*, Audit Commission, 2003.

Audit Commission, *Listen Up! Effective Community Consultation*, Audit Commission, 1999.

Our Life, Our Say (CD Rom), Young Disabled People's Forum, Greater Manchester Coalition of Disabled People, 2003.

Two Way Street (2001) – Training video and handbook for professionals about communicating with disabled children and young people. Available from: Triangle (tel: 01273 413141; www.triangle-services.co.uk; email: info@triangle-services.co.uk).

Ask Us (2002) CD Rom – a multi-media presentation of disabled children and young people's research into local services. Available from: The Children's Society, www.the-childrens-society.org.uk/bookshop.

Department of Health, Department for Education and Employment, Home Office, *Framework for the Assessment of Children in Need and their Families*, Stationery Office, 2000.

J Morris, *A Lot to Say*, SCOPE, 2002 – a guide for social workers, personal assistants and others working with disabled children and young people with communication impairment.

1.4 Consulting and involving service users

Self-evaluation checklist

Assessment and planning of services

Are children and families involved in assessments and planning their individual care and services? ■

Are children's views included in the assessment process, including those with special communication needs? ■

Do staff speak directly to children and have access to communication aids, interpreters, training, and so on, where needed? ■

Are children and families asked for their views about their care and services, and whether they feel their views have been heard? ■

Comments and complaints

Do children and families have opportunities to make comments and complaints about the services they receive? ■

Are families given information about the processes for making comments and complaints about services at first contact? ■

Are staff informed about comment and complaints procedures? ■

Are they able explain these to service users? ■

Do they show a positive attitude towards accepting users' comments? ■

Are interpretation and translation services offered where needed? ■

Involvement in strategic and service planning

Do disabled children and their families have input into service planning and high-level decision making? ■

Have consultative structures involving representatives of service users been established? ■

Are they regularly reviewed? ■

Are children and young people included as well as parents? ■

Can the needs and views of service users be shown to have a direct influence on decision making and policy development? ■

1 Planning services to meet needs

1.5 Meeting the needs of a culturally diverse population

This section will be of interest to:
✓ all service managers and frontline staff.

See also: consulting and involving service users, understanding local population and needs, understanding local services and resources.

Young people talking

Nobody should be discriminated against for who they are.

Parents talking

As Muslims, we believe strongly in religion in time of difficulty, so we would like to pray more, and we get spiritually stronger.

Neither of us had seen or heard of similar disabilities in India... We didn't know what it meant, whether we'd done something. And it made us feel badly towards Balraj, which was the worst thing. We were offered no support. It would have been good to be able to sit down with someone who understood what it was likely to mean for Balraj, and for us, and to talk through our questions and worries. But there was no-one.

I'm shy and I'm learning English... it's my third language... I used to ask a lot of questions...about what would happen next, what to expect, or how to look after him when we got him home. Eventually I gave up. I knew that if I asked them something, I'd get the same jargon answer.

She took me to [name] school which is a Catholic school. ... we are Muslim, I wouldn't mind sending her when she was 11 or 12... but at such a young age...all around you, they have Mass.

Service providers talking

We don't meet their needs. We don't address their different cultural needs.

Findings

Some of the disabled children, young people and families we spoke to faced 'double discrimination', because of their disability and ethnicity. Accounts of services' cultural sensitivity varied, ranging from families expressing gratitude that services were much better than in their country of origin to families who felt that they were effectively excluded from services that did not meet their cultural, religious and language needs.

The Race Relations (Amendment) Act 2000 strengthens and extends the Race Relations Act 1976 by placing on public authorities a new duty to promote race equality and good race relations. Alongside the Disability Discrimination Act 1995, this legislation is designed to ensure that everyone has access to the same quality of service, regardless of race or disability. However, much work still remains to be done to achieve this.

Service providers varied in their willingness and ability to respond to the needs of people from different cultures. Whereas specialist health, social services and education professionals reported that they did offer some interpreting and translation (for example, for key assessments and reviews), most mainstream services tended not to. Contrary to accepted good practice, it was common for family members, including children, to be expected to interpret or translate for other members of the family.

Some providers had designed services to meet the needs of different ethnic groups, for example, female only residential short-break schemes. However, we found that culturally appropriate services were relatively rare, and often confined only to certain cultural groups, in areas of high minority ethnic population. In other areas there was little or nothing, even by way of translation or interpreting. These findings echo other research *[see signposting]*.

Issues raised by users included:

Language and communication needs

- Lack of interpreting – at key assessments and meetings.

- Interpreters speaking the wrong dialect, or a language to an insufficient standard.

- Lack of translation of key documents, for example, letters about medical diagnosis of their child's condition, statements of special educational needs.

- Professionals' use of jargon, which could be disrespectful and effectively exclude children and parents from having a voice in decisions.

- Need for greater sensitivity around newsbreaking and presenting choices about termination of pregnancy.

- Difficulties and delays in obtaining correct diagnoses (for example, learning disability or speech problem), because language delay is wrongly attributed to bilingualism.

Cultural and religious needs

- Shortage of culturally sensitive services, for example, girls-only short breaks, appropriate food, respect for and facilitation of religious observances (for example, at school or in residential short-break schemes), placement with suitable peers.

- Lack of information about these services, where they are provided.

- Need for more workers of the same culture, or who are 'culturally competent'.

- Difficulty in making visits to country of origin, either with or without the disabled child, because of lack of reliable and appropriate short-break schemes or support.

- minority ethnic groups running their own services, funded by local authorities.

To avoid the dangers of cultural stereotyping, culturally sensitive services are tailored to local and individual needs through an understanding gained from close involvement with service users and the local community.

Providing language support for those who need it is also an important part of providing accessible, quality services. Good services:

- offer and provide interpreting at assessments and reviews for all families, whose first language is not English, in the appropriate dialect;

- offer translation of all key documents into the relevant language, where users have difficulty reading English, especially letters concerning assessments, diagnoses and service entitlement; and

- use plain, jargon-free English in meetings where there is no interpreter present, offering to repeat and explain in other terms, or to postpone the meeting until an interpreter is available.

Good practice

Tower Hamlets Families Together short-break scheme

The Families Together short-break scheme in Tower Hamlets has provided family based support for disabled children and their families (aged 0-19 yrs) for the past 16 years. The project is funded jointly by Tower Hamlets council and Barnado's. One of the key objectives of the scheme has been to meet the needs of a changing and culturally diverse community. An important principle underpinning the scheme has been to try to match children with carers of the same cultural background, wherever possible, and to provide interpreting and translation services where needed. Working closely within local community groups and building a reputation within them has meant that most minority ethnic carers are recruited by word of mouth.

From the start, the scheme looked at how to provide a multi-ethnic service in an area where the Bangladeshi community was the largest minority ethnic group. Carers were recruited from the Bangladeshi community through outreach work in a local Mosque, promoting the need for families to come forward to support disabled children. Bilingual training was then offered to potential carers, with diversity and attitudinal training essential components. Once carers were working successfully with families, they would be invited by the project to help recruit and select new carers.

To foster good ongoing relationships and networking between carers, parents and Families Together, there are annual parties and outings and plans emerging for joint training events.

Families Together employs four full-time social workers and 32 carers, who work with 40 disabled children and young people.

Critical success factors

- The project office is based in the heart of the Bangladeshi community, making it accessible to the majority ethnic group.

- The staff team reflects the community.

- Employment of Bangladeshi interpreter and translator, and bilingual reception staff, to ensure that all spoken and written communication can be bilingual.

For further information, please contact:

Jennipher Bagot (Children's Services Manager)
Tel: 0207 247 7376
Email: Jennipher.Bagot@barnardos.org.uk

Signposting

Audit Commission, *Directions in Diversity: Current Opinion and Good Practice*, Audit Commission, 2002.

Current Audit Commission research study on *Race Equality in Public Organisations*: see www.audit-commission.gov.uk/raceequality or email raceequality@audit-commission.gov.uk

T Bignall, J Butt and D Pagarani, *Something to Do: The Development of Peer Support Groups for Young Black and Minority Ethnic Disabled People*, The Policy Press, 2002.

R Flynn, *Short Breaks: Providing Better Access and More Choice for Black Disabled Children and their Parents*, The Policy Press, 2002.

Y Hussain, K Atkin and W Ahmad, *South Asian Disabled Young People and their Families*, The Policy Press, 2002

D Sachdev and A van Meeuwen (eds), *Are we Listening Yet?: Working with Minority Ethnic Communities – Some Models of Good Practice*, Barnado's, 2002.

A Vernon, *User-defined Outcomes of Community Care for Asian Disabled People*, The Policy Press, 2002.

C Hatton et al, *Supporting South Asian Families with a Child with Severe Disabilities,* Institute for Health Research, Lancaster University, 2001.

T Bignall and J Butt, *Between Ambition and Achievement: Young Black Disabled People's Views and Experiences of Independence and Independent Living,* The Policy Press, 2000.

R Chamba et al, *On the Edge: Minority Ethnic Families Caring for a Severely Disabled Child*, The Policy Press, 1999.

Self-evaluation checklist

Policies

Does the organisation/service have a clear Race Equality Scheme, covering promotion of race equality, and equality of access to goods, services, facilities and employment? ■

Is this policy translated into practical guidance and local action plans for frontline staff? ■

Is there ongoing review to monitor the effectiveness of policy implementation at local level? ■

Is there a complaints procedure, clearly advertised in different community languages, with the offer of further assistance if needed? ■

Are service users advised of local advocacy schemes that cater especially for people from different ethnic backgrounds? ■

Services

Do your services take account of the cultural needs of the local population and of particular individuals who access your service? ■

Have minority ethnic users been involved in development and evaluation of services? ■

Were both users and non-users involved? ■

Is there scope to form, support financially or refer users to local peer support groups? ■

Training

Have all staff been trained in the legal and practical implications of the Race Relations (Amendment) Act 2000? ■

Have all managers, and staff who work directly with users, received training in:

values and behaviours? ■

involving users in service design, assessments and reviews? ■

cultural and religious awareness? ■

awareness and understanding of language needs, including plain English and how to employ appropriate interpreters and translators? ■

Have opportunities for joint training with other organisations been explored? ■

Interpreting and translation

Are interpreters always offered where English is not spoken as a first language, at assessments, reviews and key meetings? ■

If not, what is the policy?

Are all key documents and information sheets translated for families who are not comfortable reading English? ■

If not, what is the policy?

How is the quality and appropriateness of the interpreting and translation assured? (right dialect, linguistic accuracy)

Are the results of consultation fed back to consultees and other service users, and outcomes explained? ■

2

The workforce

2.1 Skills, knowledge and attitudes

This section will be of interest to:
✓ managers and commissioners in all services and agencies, including voluntary sector partners.

See also: recruitment and retention, planning services to meet needs, children grow and move on.

Families talking

She was the one who got things moving, she'd come round and then she'd chat and we realised that we weren't getting the things we should have been getting. She did a lot of things that probably weren't in her job description as such... She helped with a lot of paperwork. A lot of what we've got now is down to her.

What would really have helped was somebody who knew what they were doing, not having to sit there and go through everything... it is stressful... not knowing if you will get on with that person.

Basically I felt sorry for her because she was out of her depth and a lot of the time people are just filling in for someone who's away. They walk in, they're expecting some little old man, because it says Mr X on their paper, waiting for a wash...

Services Talking

Staff skills and training have improved a lot, but what's there is child protection oriented.

We get OK support from them [nursing], but it could be better. They don't see themselves as trainers in their skills. They worry about being liable for something that goes wrong under our administration if they've trained us to do it.

Findings

Users were clear: individuals with the right knowledge, skills and attitudes can make the world of difference to their everyday lives. Families appreciated the efforts of staff striving to deliver support in a challenging and complex service system. Highly valued staff had the skills and took the time to ask disabled children and young people about their own care. They also respected parents and siblings as experts in the child's care and in their own specific needs.

We heard of many staff and service champions who clearly performed and behaved in an exceptional manner, in mainstream and specialist services. But too many users had encounters with staff who used insensitive language, ignored families' opinions or simply lacked the basic skills or confidence to deal with their children. Families found this enormously distressing and worried that some services were potentially unsafe.

Mainstream services often excluded disabled children. Commonly, children with lifting and handling needs, behavioural problems, or with more complex medical conditions were excluded, often because services were concerned about liability, or did not have the skills to include them. However, there were signs that mainstream services are preparing to meet the requirements of the Disability Discrimination Act 1995. We found that training and physical access audits were taking place across many mainstream services (for example, play, youth services and leisure), to give disabled children equal access to services and facilities. But, it was disappointing to find that in some mainstream services disability was still regarded as a marginal issue, with other 'mainstream' priorities taking clear precedence.

Unfortunately, the skills of many 'specialist' staff did not meet best practice either, with a significant proportion of disabled children being excluded even from specialist schemes, because of lack of specific skills or concerns about risk.

A few of the parents and children we spoke to had made formal complaints about their care because of poor staff skills leading to potentially unsafe practices. In every instance, complainants had been reluctant because they feared retribution or even exclusion from services, but they had acted because they felt so strongly.

Users were very consistent in the skills and attitudes they valued in staff:

- involving and consulting young people and parents about their individual care and in planning services;

- understanding a child or young person's unique abilities, disabilities and needs;

- using plain English, and age-appropriate language;

- sensitivity: using the right language at the right time;

- recognising that parents may be the 'experts' about their child;

- reliability: following through/returning calls/doing what you say you are going to do;

- honesty: if you don't know, say so – if something may not happen, don't say it will; and

- being an 'advocate' for the family and pushing on their behalf.

Users also valued staff who were able to offer good information about local services; and support based on their needs, not historical practice or inflexible protocols.

Services good at supporting and developing the right knowledge, skills and attitudes

Have management arrangements that support best skills/working practices:

- conduct locality-based staff skills reviews and incorporate results into strategic planning;

- build in time for appraisal and training – where appropriate, at multi-agency and multi-disciplinary level;

- receive proactive support from HR departments, including joint advertisement of relevant posts across agencies;

- use skills overlaps in multi-disciplinary/multi-agency teams as opportunities for role clarification and cross-speciality skill development;

- make more effective use of specialists, as a scarce resource, by piloting different configuration models (for example, for rural communities and dispersed populations by forming a network of well-informed local staff, with access to central expertise);

- recognise the importance of cascading of skills, and more flexible roles across the children's workforce (for example, for single or joint assessments, or using speech and language therapists to share their skills with learning support assistants);

- train all staff working with children in disability awareness, in mainstream and specialist services, with 'core skills' training for those working more closely with disabled children;

- find creative ways to recruit, train and supervise more carers in the community (for example, short-break foster carers) and volunteers; and

- ensure that volunteers have clear aims, roles descriptions and support

Reward and develop good people:

- review and reward good performance;

- involve users to identify staff who are performing well;

- ensure that opportunities exist for personal development and career progression;

- listen to staff ideas and support innovation/new ways of working;

- focus on developing staff skills that facilitate inclusion (for example, behaviour support, lifting and handling); and

- support and train parents and unpaid carers.

Recognise and manage the impact of service change on individuals:

- provide clear line and professional management, leadership, direction and support;

- identify and provide the skills required for joined-up working and new team relationships; and

- make time for professional skills development, clinical governance and updating expertise.

Employ staff with the right knowledge, skills and attitudes:

- staff who have excellent interpersonal skills, up-to-date professional skills, good caseload management and good team working skills;

- staff who are child-centred and age appropriate; and

- staff who are flexible and knowledgeable – demonstrating recognition and understanding of the wider service system.

Good practice

Carmarthenshire: 'Special interest groups' in the Family Aide Service

In Carmarthenshire, support in people's homes and around the community used to be provided by generic care workers who would work with any client from disabled children to older adults. Some users experienced staff who found it difficult to engage with disabled children and young people and the particular needs of their families. Sometimes, staff lacked the specialist knowledge needed to properly support families. This was distressing for the users and staff involved.

Service managers wanted to change this situation and ensure that all staff working with disabled children and young people, and their families, had the appropriate skills and knowledge to meet client needs.

They organised family support aides into a number of 'special interest groups', including a disabled children group, to share learning and develop appropriate skills as a team. Other groups were formed for parenting support and child protection; and groups share their learning with each other. The team is working to ensure that standards and good practice become more consistent. They are also focusing on sharpening their recording practices and information sharing, and improving the allocation and referral process.

The new more specialised group is also better able to respond to absences of a family's regular worker, by fielding staff with a similar skill set who already have some familiarity with the family's needs. And over time, the service manager hopes that the new roles will help with the recruitment and retention of the right kind of staff: those interested in caring and learning about this specific client group.

Managers also hope that, by offering these new posts as permanent, with more opportunities for specialised development, they will improve overall retention rates, and attract a more balanced staff profile (for example, more male workers).

Critical success factors

- Involving frontline staff in shaping and piloting the new ways of working. Changes have been carried out in full consultation with the home care aides and they have actively shaped and tested their own operational protocol.

- Establishing the more specialist group required a change of staff terms and conditions, in terms of role, and a move from sessional contracts to permanent contracts. This involved a period of tense industrial relations and close involvement with workers' unions. The service manager learned that aiming for quick change is unrealistic: this process can be difficult and time-consuming, requiring plenty of consultation time, the complete support of senior staff, and expert input from the human resource department.

- The need for new ways of working to be compatible with related services across the whole of an organisation.

For further information, please contact:

Marya Shamte (Service Manager)
Tel: 01554 745150

A place to call our own (APTCOO): Volunteer training and support

APTCOO is a voluntary sector provider of support and information services for parents and carers. They also provide training and development for carers and service providers. APTCOO are also involved in local strategic planning partnerships.

Much of APTCOO's work is supported by volunteers. Volunteers come from the local community, and include parents, students and others without a professional background in support services. It is crucial for APTCOO that the standard of information giving and other work by volunteers is consistently high. In order to achieve this and to recognise the value of people's contributions and keep volunteers motivated, APTCOO have implemented an effective performance management framework.

Critical success factors

- Volunteers have a clear agreement with APTCOO about the policies and practices that they are expected to adopt.

- Each volunteer agrees a personal plan for their time at APTCOO, setting out realistic goals and identifying the skills and experiences they wish to attain.

- Volunteers' contributions are regularly reviewed and volunteers are given frequent feedback and opportunities for further development.

For further information, please contact:

Trish Green
APTCOO
Tel: 01623 629902
Web: proweb.co.uk/~APTCOO

Signposting

Two-way Street (2001) – training video and handbook for professionals about communicating with disabled children and young people. Available from: Triangle (tel: 01273 413141; www.triangle-services.co.uk, email: info@triangle-services.co.uk).

Department of Health/Department of Education and Skills, *Together from the Start: Practical Guidance for Professionals Working with Disabled Children (Birth to Third Birthday) and their Families*, Department of Health/Department for Education and Skills, 2003.

SCOPE, *Right From the Start Template: Good Practice in Sharing the News*, SCOPE, 2003. See also: www.rightfromthestart.org.uk

G Limbrick-Spencer, *The Keyworker*, Wordworks, 2001.

Sharing Value Directory, www.sharingvalue.co.uk, provides examples and contact details for a wide range of support services which disabled children and their families have commended.

Association of Directors of Social Services, British Deaf Association, Local Government Association, National Children's Bureau, NDCS, RNID, *Deaf Children: Positive Practice Standards in Social Services*, NDCS/RNID, 2002.

Department of Health, *National Service Framework for Children* (forthcoming).

Council for Disabled Children, *Dignity and Risk*, (forthcoming 2003 guidance including lifting and handling policies and practice).

2.2 Recruitment and Retention

This section will be of interest to:
✓ managers and commissioners in all services and agencies, including voluntary sector partners.

See also: skills knowledge and attitudes, planning services to meet needs.

Families talking

When you manage to tap into something, you get a very good level of service for a while, then the person leaves and that's it.

Some nights complete strangers would turn up at the door. I never knew they were changing 'til they knocked on the door... By the time you explain how to feed him and how he chokes and things like that, it was a waste of time 'cos you get a different person the next night... And none of them had ever read the home care plan details...

Every so often we get a letter saying 'I'm your son's speech and language therapist and I will be in contact' and then you get another letter 'I am your son's speech and language therapist and I will be in contact' and I've probably got about five of those letters.

Services talking

Our staff are very committed and our best asset. It's a difficult role, to be sympathetic to client's needs and balance service demands...

The service can feel fragile for families. We accept that and worry about it. The main problem is recruitment and retention.

Reliability

- Families value stand-ins when people are away, rather than a break in services, and timely responses from services, when families have emergencies, such as a death in the family.

- When families receive support from new or covering staff, they still need the same standard of care, in terms of attitudes, skills and reliability, but often experience unacceptable variations.

- Honesty about staff availability and changes is welcomed by families: services are appreciated but often feel fragile to users due to continual staff turnover and hand-overs.

Features of good recruitment and retention policy and practice

Changes in the workforce, such as staff turnover or sickness, are inevitable. Good services do not expect users, or remaining staff, to put up with regular disruption or unreliable services. We have seen services that:

Recruit the right people:

- Attract people from the community by advertising in the right places, and presenting the right image.

- Offer regular clients to build relationships with and a 'match' of skills with needs.

- Have good support and organisation from human resources departments.

- Use joint agency advertising of relevant posts.

- Give volunteers clear aims, descriptions of their roles and support.

Retain and develop good people:

- Provide clear line management and professional management: leadership, direction and support.

- Review and reward good performance. Involve users to identify staff performing well.

- Ensure that opportunities exist for personal development and career progression.

- Listen to staff ideas and support innovation/new ways of trying things.

- Provide flexible working arrangements: job share/part-time work, crèche and childcare, and so on, to support the predominantly female workforce, who often have their own caring commitments.

Deliver robust and reliable support:

- Have good back-up systems, with changes communicated to and agreed with families.

- Keep staff briefed and equipped to meet user needs (for example, caseload sharing/core skills within the team).

Good practice

Fusion-4: Involving users in recruitment in North Nottinghamshire

Fusion-4 is a new integrated service, forming a single point of access to services for disabled children, young people and their families in North Nottinghamshire. Disabled young people, parents, carers and support workers were involved in recruiting a team co-ordinator for the new service – a key role that will have an important bearing on the way that the multi-agency service develops. In particular, disabled young people and carers wanted to ensure that the new recruit had the best possible understanding and skills for user engagement.

Users were nervous about being involved, many of them never having interviewed anyone before. Despite initial anxiety, users gained confidence throughout the recruitment day and eventually felt comfortable asking candidates questions and contributing their personal views on candidates' strengths and weaknesses.

Critical success factors

- Parents/carers felt more comfortable being part of a *panel* of interviewers, and were encouraged to bring along a friend or advocate to support them throughout the recruitment day.

- Disabled young people and parents/carers received plenty of support from the lead-recruiter in advance of the recruitment day.

- Questions were carefully selected, with candidates being asked to present to the (rather large!) panel on key issues of interest to users, such as: 'How would you ensure the ongoing involvement of disabled children, young people, their carers and families in the planning and decision making of their services?'

- Disabled young people and parents/carers were supplied with an easy-to-use candidate rating form, so they could record how well they felt the candidate answered the questions, notes about interpersonal skills, plus any other observations.

For further information, please contact:

Lesley Phair (Project Manager)
Tel: 01623 414114 (x4575)
Web: www.fusion-4.org.uk

See also:

Fusion-4 case study in section 1.3.

Signposting

Audit Commission, *Recruitment and Retention: A Public Service Workforce for the 21st Century*, Audit Commission, 2002.

This report had eleven case studies of good practice, including:

- Essex Social Services who used local media to assist with recruitment of care staff and to improve the image of working in the sector more generally;

- Dudley Social Services who recognised the importance of creating a progressive management culture to encourage staff development and retention;

- The London Borough of Lewisham who streamlined their recruitment processes to make them faster and more responsive, ensuring that the time taken to get a new person in post was minimised; and

- Blackburn, Hyndburn and Ribble Valley Healthcare NHS Trust who introduced a new approach to managing sickness absence and workplace stress that reduced staff absence and helped staff to be more honest with management about causes of stress at work.

A pocket guidebook is also available (in packs of 5) which gives a brief overview of each of the case studies and contains a 'discussion framework' - questions to help stimulate debate about how to tackle recruitment and retention in your workplace.

These Audit Commission publications are available to download from the Audit Commission's web site: www.audit-commission.gov.uk, or can be purchased by calling freephone: 0800 502030

Empower 2001: www.empower2001.org.uk - an organisation which promotes independence for disabled young people - and runs inclusive training events for disabled and non-disabled young people who want to become personal assistants.

SCOPE, *Recruiting Disabled People: Guidelines for Line Managers*, www.scope.org.uk/fast-forward/employers/recruitment.shtml

2 The workforce

2.2 Recruitment and Retention

Self-evaluation checklist

Recruitment

Do you attract and recruit the right people? ■

Do you involve disabled children, young people and their families in a range of recruitment activities? ■

> *Do you agree competencies and key skills with users?* ■

> *Do users take part in the selection of applicants to key posts, with appropriate support and preparation?* ■

Do you take measures to develop a workforce that reflects your local community profile (for example, for gender and ethnicity, and with special consideration of the value of employing disabled staff)? ■

When a post becomes vacant, do you use this as an opportunity to review the role against the skills and requirements of the job you have now (for example, hours, location, and so on)? ■

Are you actively working to attract more carers in the community (for example, short-break foster carers) and volunteers, to support the shift of services away from residential and remote service locations? ■

Retention

Do you retain and develop good people? ■

Do you train new staff and develop existing staff to cope with the specific needs of disabled children and young people and their families? ■

Do you understand your current activity and monitor the workloads of staff? ■

> *Do your staff profile their caseloads?* ■

Do you always carry out exit interviews with departing staff and take their comments seriously? ■

Do you recognise the importance of sustaining and supporting parents by providing regular training and support for them? ■

Have you implemented more flexible ways of working and support for employees (for example, flexi-time, term-time working, childcare)? ■

Planning and managing services

Do you deliver robust and reliable support? ■

Do you have, and implement, clear policies to manage sickness and absences? ■

Do your operational managers organise the daily workload of staff so that there is some flexible or floating cover in case of emergencies? ■

If necessary, do managers have agreed access to temporary staffing via a bank, and a budget to finance this? ■

If you have to change personnel at short notice, do you have back-up procedures in place to inform clients as soon as possible? ■

Do you review waiting lists and new referrals? ■

Wherever possible, do you allocate regular workers, and/or key workers, to clients, to maximise continuity of care? ■

Do operational managers encourage and monitor regular client feedback and suggestions to improve continuity and reliability? ■

Do managers identify and manage recurrent issues? ■

Do you consider recruitment and retention to be the responsibility of the whole organisation? ■

Does your human resources department work with operational teams to improve reliability and continuity? ■

Do you try to establish outcome measures for clients seen, referred elsewhere or still waiting? ■

Are agencies in your locality staffing strategically? ■

Are workforce resources being shared across the whole local service system? ■

For example, have agencies considered how playworkers, health visitors, childcare providers, nurses, learning support assistants, and so on may be able to meet some of the unmet needs of children (for example, for some therapies), with support and training from the lead professionals (for example, speech and language therapists? ■

Have you or other agencies explored the possible value of creating some generic 'child specific' support roles, with a common training for those without a background in children's services? ■

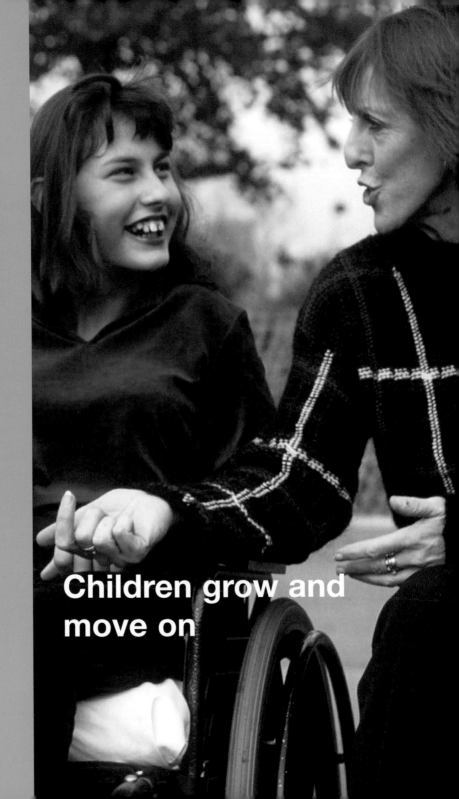

3

Children grow and move on

3.1 Early years

This section will be of interest to:
✓ doctors ✓ health visitors
✓ health professionals ✓ social
workers ✓ education
professionals ✓ childcare staff.

See also: skills knowledge and attitudes, joined-up services.

Parents talking

They were convinced, and they convinced us that he was fighting so we should fight too. They like to put the negative first so that if something happens, then it becomes a positive. They were very careful not to raise your hopes unduly at that stage and that sometimes comes across as negative, but what they were really trying to do was be realistic.

Sometimes I feel very alone. I do know that I could speak to somebody at the hospital if I wanted to talk about it. I haven't been pressurised. I could sit there and ask questions 'What's this' and 'What's going to happen' and they always left it to me. They always said 'We can talk about it again in a few months time and see how he's going'.

When we were told at the hospital it was by this young house doctor. He just came marching into the ward, didn't take me into a side room or anything and said 'Yes your daughter has Rett syndrome, she will be in a wheelchair, she will have epilepsy, sclerosis' and reeled off all the worst things, didn't say she could have it or she will have it and I just walked out the hospital thinking 'What on earth is going to happen?'

Lack of diagnosis means that it is hard to get information because you don't know what you are trying to get information on. If you wanted to meet with a support group or something, you wouldn't know which support group to meet with.

She is the health visitor, she's our friend and our co-ordinator. If I need help, she's the only person I would turn to. I would tell her anything. She helped me fill all my forms in, we had so much in our heads… Everything we had to find out we did through her, she came and did everything at home, it was a lot of help.

Findings

During a disabled child's early years, the child and family have a number of key experiences:

- finding out about the child's condition;

- getting a full diagnosis;

- establishing contact with services; and

- provision of childcare and early education.

It is important that parents are initially informed of their child's disability in a sympathetic, informative and supportive way. Studies such as Right from the Start *[see signposting]* have identified the long-term damage done to parents and children by insensitivity and poor communication. It is disappointing that a number of families who took part in our study described unsympathetic and unhelpful experiences of first hearing about their child's disability. These included being told in a public ward; being told in jargon that they could not understand; and being given an unnecessarily negative picture of their child's condition. Some also described unsympathetic attitudes from professionals in relation to decisions about termination of pregnancy, particularly where the family's culture or beliefs made this a sensitive issue.

Some parents described more positive experiences. In particular, they valued being given the time to take in the information about their child's disability, and being invited to go back with questions if they could not take it all in at once. They appreciated staff taking a positive attitude, and at the same time welcomed the honesty of those who let them know what the worst outcome might be.

Parents often experienced long delays in diagnosis, during which they were sometimes referred from one professional to another, with no single case file to record all the information about their child. If there was no proper inter-agency referral system in place, parents were obliged to go round different professionals themselves, telling the story of their child's condition over and over again.

A common difficulty around the lack of a clear diagnosis was that it made it difficult for families to access information and services. In some cases, even when a child is obviously disabled, it takes time to clarify exactly what condition he or she has. But some of the families we spoke to felt that their early awareness of their child's symptoms had not been taken seriously. Families also pointed out that benefits, support and information are often dependent on having a clear diagnosis, and felt that they were being denied help simply because of the lack of a named condition. But even families with a diagnosis frequently experienced difficulties with finding out what services were available, and what services and benefits they were entitled to, as information was not available from a single place or individual.

Another early concern for parents was the lack of childcare facilities suitable for disabled children. Research has shown that looking after a disabled child is more expensive, yet parents of disabled children are more likely to struggle to work because of the lack of suitable affordable childcare, and get caught in a poverty trap. Children also miss out on opportunities to develop skills and mix with other children.

Some disabled children may benefit from specialised childcare. But many could be looked after in mainstream services, but are denied places for a number of reasons:

- lack of staff to provide extra time or care for the child;

- lack of staff trained in caring for disabled children;

- staff being unwilling or unable to meet child's needs (for example, giving medication); and

- restrictive lifting and handling policies.

Whilst the National Childcare Strategy aims to make quality affordable childcare available for disabled children from 0-16, there is currently very little available for disabled children, whether special or inclusive. In disadvantaged areas, the Sure Start programme can make funding available to provide more childcare places.

The National Service Framework for Children is likely to emphasise the need for more sensitive and joined-up early years services for disabled children and their families.

Key features of a good service

Early support and information are vital for parents who are finding out about a child's disability, so health, childcare and early education professionals are trained to take proactive steps to identify disability and special educational needs as early as possible. Parents' concerns are always taken seriously. Once a diagnosis has been reached, it is shared with the parents immediately.

Health and other professionals who are likely to be closely involved in giving information about a child's diagnosis receive regular communication skills training in giving news and information sensitively.

Key factors in supporting parents when giving them information about their child's condition include:

- the environment where this takes place – privacy is important;

- showing sensitivity and empathy;

- avoiding technical terms and jargon;

- offering written as well as verbal information;

- giving parents time to absorb information, and encouraging them to come back with questions afterwards;

- being honest about what is not known yet about the child's condition;

- being positive about the future, without hiding the problems;

- giving information about other local services (for example, childcare, family support, benefits); and

- giving information about local or national support groups.

Assessments are co-ordinated, for example, through the development of joint or multi-disciplinary assessment processes, which help to build a whole picture of the child and avoid families having to attend repeated assessments by different professionals. This also speeds up diagnosis and the provision of services that follow it. A keyworker system helps to co-ordinate the reaching of a diagnosis and the provision of services from different agencies. This is particularly important before a child reaches school age, when the special educational needs process can help to provide service co-ordination. The case study below gives an example of a service co-ordination pilot scheme.

Services – including benefits, housing, equipment, health, home care assistance, and therapies – are put in place as soon as possible after assessment. If reaching a full diagnosis will take some time, appropriate services are provided in the interim. There is a 'one stop shop' approach to information about services and benefits for all families with disabled children, including voluntary sector support groups.

The Early Years Development and Childcare Partnership (EYDCP) ensures that parents of disabled children are consulted in audits of local childcare, and supports providers in moving towards inclusion of all children, as well as fostering more specialist provision, where needed. The case study in section 4.2 shows how an inclusive 'playcare' model was developed by a local authority, and adopted by an EYDCP, to successfully prepare play and childcare settings to include more disabled children.

Good practice

Service co-ordination project for children under eight with complex needs in Leicester

The scheme has been overseen from the start in 1998 by a multi-agency steering group, comprising representatives from health, social services, education and the voluntary sector, across three local authority areas. Parents sit on the steering group. The scheme depends on the continuing commitment of financial resources from all the agencies involved, which is done through a complex multi-agency funding arrangement, including HIMP.

The philosophy behind the scheme is to empower parents and provide a framework to allow them to speak to multiple professionals and agencies effectively. There are three main co-ordinating mechanisms:

- regular service planning meetings between families and the multi-disciplinary team, organised around the child;

- use of a keyworker – a professional or parental service co-ordinator – who is nominated by parents themselves; and

- use of parent-held multi-agency service plans and records.

A cultural linkworker can join the team to help professionals to understand a family's cultural needs. The linkworker can also be chosen by families to act as their service co-ordinator.

From a small pilot project this scheme is now being extended to other areas in the locality, as well as to children over eight. The scheme has received national recognition as a good practice model, as well as strong positive evaluation from parents and professionals.

Critical success factors:

- Open and comprehensive information sharing between families and agencies involved, with explicit written parental agreement.

- A lead person, who is appointed through a multi-agency system, and provides consistent input and maintenance.

- Multi-agency:
  - funding and management;
  - commitment and impetus;
  - monitoring;
  - agreement and clarity about the co-ordination mechanisms;
  - unambiguous eligibility criteria; and

- input for keyworkers/co-ordinators.

- A 'spirit of goodwill' and sense of equal partnership among the agencies, and with families.

For more information, please contact:

Anette Beattie (Project Manager)
Specialist Community Child Health Services
Bridge Park Plaza, Bridge Park Road, Leicester, LE4 8PQ
Tel: 0116 223 2427
Email: Anette.Beattie@lcwpct.nhs.uk

Signposting

Department of Health/Department for Education and Skills, *Together from the Start: Practical Guidance for Professionals Working with Disabled Children (birth to third birthday) and their Families*, Department of Health/Department for Education and Skills, 2003.

SCOPE, *Right from the Start Template: Good Practice in Sharing the News*, SCOPE, 2003. See also: www.rightfromthestart.org.uk

A Leonard, *Right from the Start*, SCOPE, 1999.

Daycare Trust, *Ambitious for All: Rising to the Challenge for Children with Disabilities and Special Needs* (Policy Paper 5), Daycare Trust, 2001.

Department of Health, *National Service Framework for Children* (forthcoming)

Council for Disabled Children, *Dignity and Risk* (2003, forthcoming guidance including lifting and handling policies and practice).

Self-evaluation checklist

Is the diagnostic process co-ordinated and streamlined? ■

If there are difficulties and delays, what steps are being taken towards quicker, more effective diagnoses?

Are case notes shared between professionals? ■

Are agencies working to develop joint assessments? ■

Does one individual have responsibility for co-ordinating different professional consultations and getting a diagnosis for the child? ('keyworker') ■

Are parents given clearly written letters and clear verbal information throughout the process? ■

Is a full diagnosis made and shared with parents as soon as possible? ■

Are services made available to families before diagnosis? ■

Are parents informed about their child's condition in a sensitive and supportive way? ■

Are staff across all disciplines trained in how to give information about disability? ■

Are parents given news about disability in a private space? ■

Do staff have time to explain fully and answer parents' questions? ■

Are parents given a point of contact for further information and questions? ■

Have parents been asked about their experiences of finding out about their child's condition? ■

If problems have been identified, are steps being taken to address their concerns? ■

Are parents given support and information in the child's early years? ▪

Do services offer proactive, co-ordinated support to respond to the needs of children and families before and after diagnosis? ▪

Do families have a single point of contact for information and advice? ▪

Are families given details of support groups and voluntary organisations? ▪

Does this include organisations that are not condition-specific, prior to diagnosis? ▪

Can all families with disabled children who want it access affordable good quality childcare? ▪

Are places in mainstream childcare available for disabled children? ▪

If not, are the criteria for gaining a place being reviewed? ▪

Are places available to disabled children being taken up? ▪

If not, have the reasons been reviewed and steps taken to address them? ▪

Do mainstream childcare facilities take steps to make disabled children welcome and avoid stereotyping? ▪

Are specialised facilities available for children who need them? ▪

Do parents have access to information about childcare facilities and which ones are suitable for their child? ▪

Does the EYDCP actively support the expansion of suitable childcare for disabled children? ▪

Does the EYDCP have a disability/special needs subgroup, or an equal opportunities subgroup? ▪

Does the EYDCP carry out audits of local childcare needs? ▪

Has the EYDCP carried out an access audit? ▪

Are goals and targets for take-up of childcare by disabled children being set and met? ▪

3 Children grow and move on

3.1 Early years

Do childcare staff have training in caring for disabled children, and disability awareness training? ■

Are all available funding streams being accessed, including Sure Start? ■

Are services working together towards implementation of the National Service Framework for Children? ■

3.2 Services designed for children and young people

This section will be of interest to:
✓ all staff working with and managing services for disabled children and their families.

See also: consulting and involving service users, early years, moving into adulthood, play and leisure, equipment, transport, the workforce.

Children and young people talking

It's good, there is a waiting room with toys and books and newspapers, and the people in the hospital are nice.

I don't like waiting – I like it when it's got toys.

Parents talking

There is plenty of money for children who are born like this but they didn't have any money for children of her age.

They find it difficult to mix him with the right age group and the right abilities and they feel that as he is getting a bit older it is getting more difficult to do that with him so they wanted us to find somewhere else. So I phoned up social services and there is nothing.

You've got to chase them all the time and there's no service actually there for you…The life span of children with CP [cerebral palsy] is not as long as ordinary children. I think that children that have got conditions like that, to make their and their parents' life easier it would be a lot better if the services were a lot quicker to save a lot of that heartache…

They are lovely lovely ladies, but would a 16-year-old boy choose to go out with two women in their late 50s, he wouldn't, would he? And I said that they should be looking for more appropriate carers, somebody younger, or more in tune with the sort of things Pete wants, but again they never came up with anybody.

Siblings talking

It helps you grow up a lot. You can't just be a kid.

Findings

A child- and family-centred approach means designing services to meet their needs, rather than fitting families to services. Although needs differ depending on disability and family circumstances, there are some common principles about designing services that are appropriate to children rather than adults.

Children's physical, emotional and social needs change and so do their needs for services (for example, moving from primary to secondary school, play to youth services). There are critical periods for physical growth or language acquisition. Waiting times carry more significance for children than adults. The way children and young people communicate and express themselves develops rapidly over time.

The Kennedy report made a large number of recommendations concerning the future organisation of health services for children, stressing the importance of their particular needs, as children. The National Service Framework for Children will set multi-agency standards for disabled children's services.

While some services set out to cater for children and young people's needs, for example, play or youth services, many services are still primarily geared towards adults, or do not take account of the particular needs of children and families. Service providers we spoke to were aware that often services needed to be more child and family friendly. However, families' experiences indicated that there is still some way to go with many services.

Children appreciated staff who related to them as children...

He [short-break carer] does press-ups and claps his hands while he's in the air. He's really funny.

and professionals who took them seriously and explained what was happening, in an age-appropriate and sensitive way:

When my bro' was sick in intensive care, as brothers and sisters we were told about the condition my brother had... so we knew what was happening to him.

Families reported the following common difficulties in their encounters with staff:

- Professionals who did not involve children and/or parents respectfully in reviews or medical consultations.

- Staff who did not relate appropriately to children, including the need to be playful or provide age-appropriate explanations or consent processes.

- Lack of continuity of staff, which often made it impossible to be sensitive to an individual child or family's needs.

- Carers or befrienders who did not match a young person's developmental needs (for example, a disabled young man's preference for a male carer).

In relation to services, parents reported:

- Gaps in services for children of particular ages – for example, between the end of play services and the start of youth services.

- Gaps in local services, for children with certain support needs, making it difficult for them to have any local friends.

- Long waiting lists, rapid turnover and shortages of key staff, (for example, speech and language therapists, physiotherapists, occupational therapists).

- Slow provision of community and education equipment.

- Lack of behaviour support services (for example, sleep patterns, dealing with aggression, sexuality).

- Lack of opportunities for disabled young people to have regular contact with both disabled and non-disabled peer groups, outside school, as part of social development.

- Services which were not age-appropriate (for example, for young people with learning disabilities – disabled young people criticised waiting areas full of baby toys).

- Service barriers to gaining increased independence in adolescence (for example, transport).

- Adverse impact on family income and quality of life, due to lack of service co-ordination (for example, multiple assessments and appointments during school and working hours, and lack of reliable childcare and after school/holiday provision).

Some of these issues are covered in more detail in other sections of the handbook.

Key features of child and family friendly services

User involvement and consultation is central to everyday working practices, as well as continuous service review and development. The needs of parents, carers and siblings are considered alongside those of the child *[see section 1.4]*.

There is a strategic approach to service planning across different providers, and co-ordinated service delivery, with facilities for children and young people of all ages and needs, whether this is play and leisure, childcare, education, health or social care.

Education, health and social services assessments and appointments are arranged to fit in with children's and families' time commitments, and co-ordinated through a keyworker arrangement where appropriate, to maximise effective multi-disciplinary working and prevent families from being overburdened with different appointments.

All staff working with disabled children – in mainstream and specialist services – are trained in working with children, and are able to meet their developmental and communication needs. They also communicate clearly and sensitively with parents, carers and siblings. Joint training initiatives share and cascade skills across organisations. Recruitment and retention initiatives are developed to improve quality and continuity of carers, learning support assistants, and other staff.

Professional shortages are identified, and measures taken to minimise the potential adverse implications for children. For example, there are clear criteria for caseload prioritisation, and use of specialists to train others (for example, teachers, learning support assistants, carers and parents) to work with children who are on waiting lists *[see section 2.2]*.

Waiting times for community and education equipment are regularly monitored and steps taken to reduce delays which are likely to be detrimental to a child's development or quality of life *[see section 4.4]*.

Good practice

Leicester Royal Infirmary: Role of playworking in children's services

Leicester Royal Infirmary has a team of 30 qualified playworkers, who provide services across all children's areas of the hospital, including outpatients, child development centre, admissions, all children's wards, neonatal unit, intensive care unit, accident and emergency department. Services are provided in most areas of the hospital seven days a week, 365 days a year. All staff have basic NNEB or BTEC childcare qualifications, and most have completed the hospital play specialist course (HPSET).

Hospital playworkers:

- prepare children for procedures/surgery through play or age-appropriate explanation (for example, taking blood from dolly, role play, pictures, slides);

- keep children calm or distracted during treatment (for example, A&E, placement of canula);

- provide post-procedural play or explanation (for example, what happened in a road traffic accident);

- create a friendly environment so that children and adolescents feel settled in hospital and have interesting things to fill their time, especially long-stay patients;

- help children to meet developmental milestones and prevent regression;

- carry out rehabilitation (with occupational therapists); and

- educate medical students, other clinical staff and parents.

There are inclusive playrooms in every area of the hospital, a multi-sensory room (for disabled and very sick children to relax), and adolescent rooms attached to a number of wards. All playspaces indoors and outdoors are accessible to all children, including those in wheelchairs or in beds. Age-appropriate play equipment is provided – so that older children with learning disabilities, for example, do not have to use baby toys. Children are integrated socially and physically as much as possible, for example, tube-fed children are encouraged to sit with their peers at the meal table.

With longer stays in hospital, children and young people are fully involved in a multi-disciplinary assessment that looks at the whole child and contributes to a daily plan, where there is dedicated playtime, as well as set times for medical routines, meals, and therapies.

Critical success factors

- Integration of playworking into all aspects of a child's hospital visit or stay.

- Commitment of clinical staff to inclusion of playworkers as essential part of multi-disciplinary team.

For further information, please contact:

Tina Clegg
Tel: 0116 258 6173
Email: tina.clegg@uhl-tr.nhs.uk

Signposting

Two Way Street (2001) – training video and handbook for professionals about communicating with disabled children and young people. Available from Triangle [Tel: 01273 413141; www.triangle-services.co.uk].

Ask Us (2002) CD Rom – a multi-media presentation of disabled children and young people's research into local services. Available from: The Children's Society – www.the-childrens-society.org.uk/bookshop.

National Association of Hospital Play Staff: www.nahps.org.uk

I Kennedy, *Learning from Bristol: The Report of the Public Enquiry into Children's Heart Surgery at the Bristol Royal Infirmary 1984-1995*, Bristol Royal Infirmary Enquiry, 2001.

Department of Health, *National Service Framework for Children*, (forthcoming).

DCMS, *Beyond 2004 – A DCMS Framework for Action on Disability*, DCMS, 2003.

Self-evaluation checklist

Seamless services

Is there a strategic forum where different specialist and mainstream agencies plan seamless services for disabled children? ■

Or is there work towards one? ■

Has there been a recent review that looked at families' needs and priorities for services compared to existing services? ■

Has there been a recent mapping exercise of local services that covered age, eligibility criteria, type of impairment, specialist/inclusive services, locality, and transition arrangements? ■

What gaps were identified and what is the impact on families?

What were the reasons for the gaps and what is being done to fill them?

What choices are provided for children and young people in terms of local social and leisure activities?

Were disabled children and young people involved in choosing these? ■

Is there a local guide to services to help families 'navigate the system'? ■

Does it identify:

Appropriate summer play schemes for a disabled child? ■

Suitable leisure centres for young people with autism? ■

What signposting are agencies and their staff able to provide for families?

Do families find it easy to find out what is available? ■

What have they found helpful/unhelpful?

Communicating with children and young people

Have all staff who come into contact with disabled children and young people been trained in talking to children and young people in an age-appropriate way, which meets any specific communication needs relating to their disability? ■

Has this training involved contact with disabled children and young people, including feedback from them on how they like to be involved in services and spoken with? ■

What do children and young people feel about how they are involved in assessments, reviews and clinic appointments?

Do they feel well informed and respected? ■

Did they feel they had a say, in an environment that felt safe? ■

Did they understand and feel comfortable with the language being used? ■

If there are differences between the views of the child and the views of the parent or other family members, how are these dealt with in decisions about services?

Have you involved disabled children and young people in service design? (For example, in the design of waiting areas or youth club activity programmes.) ■

Were children and young people with different types of disability involved? ■

Including those with higher levels of support need for example, specific or complex communication needs? ■

And learning disability? ■

Have the children and young people who participated been told what staff have done to improve services as a result of the consultation? ■

Waiting times and staffing

How long do people have to wait for services (for example, therapies, short breaks)?

_____

How are cases prioritised?

_____

How is fairness ensured?

_____

What, if any, steps are being taken to offer support to those who are not currently able to access services?

_____

Have local standards and targets been developed for waiting times for:

acute interventions for children? ■

provision of therapies? ■

equipment? ■

housing adaptations? ■

Do these targets meet families' needs? ■

How are services performing against local targets?

_____

How are local services working towards the implementation of the National Service Framework for Children?

_____

What measures are in place to ensure that appointments, assessments and reviews are at times that cause minimum disruption to families and their other commitments?

Are any steps being taken to minimise waiting times on the day (for example, in clinics)?

Staffing

What steps are being taken to ensure continuity of staff, wherever possible?

Do families/young people have any choice about regular care staff?

What happens if they do not establish a positive rapport with a carer?

3.3 Moving into adulthood

This section will be of interest to:
✓ all staff who work with or manage services for disabled young people.

See also: family support, joined-up services.

Young people talking

The Link course is good because you get to choose what you want to do...

I hate being spoken to through my parents. If they want to speak to me, speak to me, not anybody else... people tend to think I am a lot less intelligent than I am. That is one of the big problems, a very big problem.

Parents talking

When she leaves school she is going to find it hard, because in school at the moment it is very friendly, like home...

When she had her annual review at 14 that was when they first discussed it and a few professionals came along and since then we have heard nothing at all... I know that each year something should be mentioned about transition at the review but this just doesn't happen – they didn't mention it at all.

I've read stuff about you having a key person and I never felt that I had a key person to talk to... I guess in a sense that it might have been a social worker... I never thought he was fighting my corner... It was horrid, horrid.

...the people were all too old, aged in their forties, and this is not the right environment for a girl of 18. Residential homes for 18-65, that's not right... It's got to be somewhere with young people...with a pub round the corner and shops nearby. I didn't want her stranded in the middle of nowhere...she wants to be able to go out.

The change over must be gradual. He can only take little steps at a time, as he retains the familiarity as he moves onto something new. He can't cope with a sudden change.

Findings

Young people's views

Disabled young people in our research said they wanted more choices, better joint working between agencies and the chance to become more independent from their families. They felt that professionals needed to understand both their capabilities and needs better, so that, for example, they might have a stretching but suitably supported opportunity to go to college or find a work placement. They also stressed the importance of professionals being available to help them plan for their social and leisure time.

Many young people said that they were looking forward to their college placement or new adult placement. However, there were also a substantial number who were experiencing frustration because of:

- Poor information about opportunities and services.

- Lack of attractive options open to young disabled adults.

- Professional advisers lacking understanding of their needs and aspirations.

- Difficulties obtaining realistic advice about the genuine willingness of colleges to support and include them – some had had to leave their course as a result.

Many disabled young people planned to carry on living at home because of lack of suitable supported living arrangements, although parents were concerned that this would not be a long-term solution. Some young people and their parents were interested in the idea of employing carers through direct payments, which would at least give them some greater choice over their lives; however, a few reported ambivalent attitudes on the part of social services departments.

Parents' views

There was a spectrum of parental experience, from those who were satisfied with the adult provision planned and had few anxieties, to those who had had to battle for agencies to take an interest and work together to plan ahead.

Amongst parents a very common concern was how their child would cope in a very different, less protective adult environment, following years of attending the same school, with the same friends, familiar staff and routines. Parents emphasised the need to move a young person across gradually into an adult environment, with maximum opportunities for them to visit new establishments, make informed choices and meet new staff.

Many families reported difficulties in engaging agencies in transition planning, despite a requirement to do so for young people with special educational needs. Often agencies did not offer coherent arrangements for moving into adult services or away from home, because of poor collaboration. Many parents commented that the professionals advising them and their child did not appear to have an understanding of the young person's abilities and needs, as well as a realistic understanding of the provision available and how suitable support could be organised. Often there was no transport or practical support offered to visit potential colleges or residential homes.

Parents sometimes felt pressured into accepting unsuitable placements, which they believed were probably offered more for administrative or financial reasons than to meet their child's needs. They felt they had to battle against professionals' plans. Visits to some proposed adult residential or daycare establishments left parents with the impression that no care had been taken to assess their suitability – for example, an isolated unit with much older people, or a placement with people with severe behavioural disorders for a young person with a physical disability.

Many parents said that they would have valued a key worker or advocate, who could have helped them to get the most appropriate provision for their child. They would also have valued information about the whole range of options at a much earlier stage, to give them time to explore them properly with their child, and be in a stronger position to assess the advice given by professionals. There was also often a lack of information about child and parental eligibility for benefits and services, as they changed across different age thresholds.

Features of a good transitions service

Agencies providing an effective transitions service for young people:

- have a clear and agreed multi-agency process where professionals undertake joint planning for the young person's needs, preferences and options, from year nine;

- are committed to person-centred planning and working towards its implementation;

- involve disabled young people and their families in the design and evaluation of transitions services (for example, through Connexions partnerships and Learning Disability Partnership Boards);

- have staff who are trained in disability awareness and in communicating with disabled young people, who understand the needs of young people with different types of disabilities, and the range of local service options available for them;

- plan for and provide a range of suitable local adult services, including education, employment, leisure, housing, health and social care, to meet needs and aspirations;

- provide accessible, timely information for users about adult services and any benefits to which they could be entitled (including Braille versions, large print, Makaton, and so on);

- provide practical assistance to help disabled young people and their families to visit and assess potential colleges or other establishments; and

- involve respectfully and empower (for example, through offering independent advocacy) the young disabled person, and his or her family, in decision making.

Direct payments for social care services represent an important option for some young people who wish to take more control over how and by whom their care is provided. User-friendly schemes are well advertised locally, promoted by other professionals in contact with disabled young people, and offer good initial and ongoing support.

Offers of adult residential placements take account of the key considerations for parents and young people:

- quality of care staff;

- pleasantness and cleanliness of facility;

- ability of facility to meet specific needs (for example, communication, equipment, therapy);

- compatibility with other clients – age, disability, gender;

- location and need to retain proximity to friends and family;

- opportunity to take part in community life (not physically or socially isolated); and

- availability of interesting activities, shops and pubs, in the nearby area.

Agencies working towards more effective transitions do so within the Connexions partnerships, and work closely with Learning Disability Partnership Boards. Frameworks and protocols are tailored for disabled young people and suitably trained staff act as their advisers. The National Service Framework for Children is likely to stress the need for better multi-agency working at transition.

- Listening and responding to users' unmet needs and working with other agencies to meet them.

For further information, please contact:

John McConnell (Strategic Planning Manager)
Tel 01752 307340
Email: john.mcconnell@plymouth.gov.uk

Signposting

Getting a Life - a three year project set up by the Council for Disabled Children to identify good and innovative practice in transitions planning for young people with learning disabilities. Helen Wheatley (tel: 020 7843 6446), Hwheatley@ncb.org.uk

Trans-active - a MENCAP project promoting the idea of a multi-media transition 'passport', developed in pairs by young people with learning disabilities with non-disabled peers. Resource materials for teachers and website available, www.trans-active.org.uk

Contact a Family, *Transition in England and Wales Factsheet*, Contact a Famliy, 2002. www.cafamily.org.uk, tel: 020 7608 8700

National Centre for Independent Living, *Direct Payments - A Beginners Guide* (video), www.ncil.org.uk, tel: 020 7587 1663.

Living it Up (newsletter/CD Rom written by disabled young people for other young people at transition.) Available from Norah Fry Research Centre, tel: 0117 923 8137 www.bris.ac.uk/Depts/NorahFry/Transition/livingitup1.pdf

Department of Health, *National Service Framework for Children* (forthcoming).

Joseph Rowntree Foundation have published a number of reports on transitions to adulthood: www.jrf.org.uk

Self-evaluation checklist

Strategic partnerships

Are disabled young people involved in the development of
transition services, for example:

*through the local Connexions partnership business planning
process and Youth Charter?* ■

through the Learning Disability Partnership Board? ■

Are those with high-level support needs and special
communication needs also involved? ■

Are Connexions personal advisers and other transition workers
trained to work with disabled young people? ■

Are agencies committed to the development of person-centred
planning? ■

*Have agencies made progress in implementing person-centred
planning for all disabled young people moving from children's to
adults' services* ■

Are agencies working together towards the implementation of
the National Service Framework for Children? ■

Multi-agency assessments

Do all young people with SEN have a multi-agency transition
plan at year nine review? ■

And is this updated at each subsequent review? ■

Do all relevant professionals attend annual reviews? ■

If not how do they contribute?

How are young people and their families empowered to
contribute to their reviews?

Is there one place where disabled young people can get all the help that they need for transition planning? ■

Is there any generally available information about the transition process and how service and benefits entitlements and arrangements change across the age range? ■

Are there any joint assessment protocols for disabled young people at transition? ■

How well are they working?

Is a range of realistic options presented to each disabled young person, suited to their needs? ■

Do transition assessments consider leisure and social needs? ■

How are young people in care assisted to make choices?

Who checks and is responsible for follow through?

Apart from the young person and their family, who will notice if the agreed plans fail to be delivered or a placement turns out to be unsuitable?

Choices

Do young people have a choice to live independently? ■

Is adequate support available? ■

If shared or residential accommodation is offered:

is this with other people of a similar age? ■

is it local to friends and family, if this is important to the young person? ■

is there an understanding of and ability to meet specific needs? ■

is transport available to shops and other outside activities? ■

Is there a well-publicised user-friendly direct payments scheme in operation locally? ■

Do disabled young people have the option of a work placement, or vocational training that could realistically lead to work? ■

What measures are there to ensure that colleges can meet the specific needs of a disabled young person, and that the social environment is truly inclusive?

What assistance is given to disabled young people, particularly those with communication, sensory or mobility needs, to visit colleges and make informed choices?

What help is available for the young person if a placement turns out not to be suitable?

Are young people made aware of any local advocacy scheme and how to access it? ■

What arrangements are there to meet cultural, religious and language needs of young people at transition?

4

Inclusion in everyday life

4 Inclusion in everyday life

This section will be of interest to:
✓ Local Education Authority officers ✓ Special Educational Needs Co-ordinators
✓ headteachers ✓ class teachers ✓ learning support assistants.

See also: skills knowledge and attitudes, recruitment and retention, moving into adulthood, equipment, transport.

Children and young people talking

It's nice. I've got friends there...They come on the same bus.

The question is why not? I want one [an adapted computer] but you just have to wait.

Parents talking

The time it takes, it's very agonising for the parents. They say that children can access the same type of services at school as other children but I don't think that is a very fair way of putting it basically...There is a huge struggle, of reviews, and this, that, and the other.

The fact that it really needed a multi-disciplinary assessment and she's never had that...the only times the different disciplines have talked to each other is when I've nagged them into doing it, which I think is wrong. I find it amazing that it's not set up already. I still don't understand why health and education can't talk to each other.

The professionals like to take over and put their point across on what they want to do, and they do sometimes forget that he is our child, and we can have a say in what happens to him...

You can quickly establish whether advice is based on what does least damage to their budget, and when it is based on what is best for Simon.

Siblings talking

Our Brian gets bullied in school – they call him names and push him. He's very shy, he doesn't like telling.

- was included in the whole life of the school (sport, outings).

Parents commonly reported the following weakness in services, many of which were also mentioned by children and young people themselves:

- long waits for assessments, often followed by long delays for services or equipment;

- lack of multi-disciplinary or joint assessments, and absence of keyworking to facilitate inter-agency working;

- inappropriate or distant placements for particular needs (for example, autism);

- reluctance of LEAs/schools to address parental concerns about placements;

- severe delays and shortages in therapy provision (for example, speech and language, physiotherapy, occupational therapy);

- rapid turnover of therapists and LSAs;

- frequent attitudinal and physical barriers (such as ramps, lifts and toilets) to placement in mainstream schools and a perceived reluctance to make adjustments; and

- the extent of bullying within mainstream schools: with many parents seeing a special school placement as the only realistic alternative.

There was also a perception that more articulate parents, or those who 'shouted loudest', received more favourable treatment for their child.

The experience of being involved in annual reviews varied, with some parents enjoying the opportunity to take part in setting and measuring objectives, and hearing professionals take an interest in their child. However, there were also negative experiences, where parents told us about:

- professionals who dismissed their in-depth knowledge of their child's needs, or spoke in a professional jargon, which excluded them;

- repeated discussions and reviews of their child's needs (often by new professionals who had no prior knowledge of their child), with little follow through;

- absence of key professionals from reviews;

- proposals apparently driven by cost considerations or administrative convenience;

- absence of community language interpreting and translation;

- parents or children excluded from reviews due to inaccessible venue; and

- difficulties of engaging schools and other agencies in transition planning for adult services *[see section 3.3]*.

Key features of a good service

Education services that meet the social and educational needs of disabled children and young people have the following arrangements in place:

- Timely assessment and provision for needs, at School Action Plus, or through a statement of special educational needs (SEN).

- Appropriate involvement of parents and children in assessments and reviews, with plain English used in meetings and in written communications.

- Interpreters offered where needed and written material translated.

- Accessibility plans for mainstream schools (SEN and Disability Act 2001).

- Suitable local provision for children with all types of special educational need, to avoid the need to go to residential school, or to travel long distances.

- Training of all teaching and learning support staff in disability awareness and core skills for working with children with SEN (for example, curriculum differentiation, behaviour management), especially in mainstream schools.

- A pool of staff trained in particular specialisms (such as British Sign Language, autism and so on), supported by a strategy to promote effective recruitment and retention (for example, for LSAs).

- Proactive disability awareness work with pupils within mainstream schools, to encourage acceptance and prevent bullying of disabled pupils.

Agencies undertake joint planning through the development of multi-agency strategic planning forums, shared electronic databases, formal information sharing agreements and pooled budgets (for example, for equipment).

The LEA promotes inclusive practice, through:

- establishing effective strategic partnership working, with parents, voluntary organisations and other agencies;

- developing the capacity of schools to respond to diverse pupil needs; and

- supporting continuous self-improvement through effective monitoring arrangements.

Many of the key issues raised above are addressed in much fuller detail in the Audit Commission's two recent reports on SEN, and the self-review handbook *[see signposting]*.

The DfES has announced a new SEN Action Programme, which is to be published in 2003. It will aim to help all children with SEN to reach their potential by:

- improving access to education;

- raising standards of teaching and learning; and

- strengthening partnerships with children, parents and carers.

Our research covered children in mainstream and special day schools. Children in residential schools were not specifically included, but references are given in the Signposting section to recent research on their needs and experiences.

 Good practice

Tower Hamlets: Making children with SEN feel welcome at Bangabandhu school

Bangabandu School is a community primary school in Tower Hamlets. Since the school opened 13 years ago, it has actively sought to include children with SEN, some with significant disabilities. The school has a highly inclusive ethos and much care is taken to help children to settle in and make friends. A number of different approaches are used, including:

Establishing a 'circle of friends'

The Special Educational Needs Co-ordinator (SENCO), who has been trained in this technique, will ask a child who appears to be having difficulty making friends if they would like to try this approach. Classmates are invited to volunteer to be part of their circle, which will then meet weekly to plan how they will work and play together. For each child, the scheme involves an hour a week of a SENCO's time, to bring the circle of friends together and help them play together, over 10-12 weeks. At present the scheme is limited to only three children a year, because of the SENCO's other commitments. However, there are plans to train a classroom assistant in the technique, so that the number of children benefiting can rise to six per year.

Paired reading

Children with SEN are carefully paired with other pupils to read together – helping to increase their confidence and improve their reading. Older children who are struggling with reading have helped younger pupils to learn; and younger ones who are reading to a standard well above their age have worked with older pupils. Whole classes have also been paired to read together.

Encouraging classmates to welcome disabled pupils

Classmates are encouraged to welcome children whose physical or behavioural difficulties might otherwise set them apart. For example, when two children with complex needs were joining the school, future classmates volunteered to meet them in advance and then played an active role in helping them to settle in. In other cases, families have shared photos and teachers have explained to classmates that a child might look or act a bit differently, but that they should make an extra effort to make them feel welcome.

Critical success factors

All staff and children who will have contact with a new disabled child are prepared in advance to include him or her positively. The SENCO, class teacher or the head facilitate this process.

For further information, please contact:

Cathy Philips (Headteacher)
Email: head@bangabandhu.towerhamlets.sch.uk

Signposting

Audit Commission, *Statutory Assessment and Statements of SEN: In Need of Review?*, Audit Commission, 2002.

Audit Commission, *Special Educational Needs: A Mainstream Issue*, Audit Commission, 2002.

Web based products at www.audit-commission.gov.uk:

- Self-review handbook for LEAs (2002)

- Online ideas directory (case studies of effective LEA practice)

- Review of academic literature by Institute of Education, University of London

D Abbott, J Morris and L Ward, *Disabled Children and Residential Schools: A Study of Local Authority Policy and Practice*, Norah Fry Research Centre, 2000.

DfES, *SEN Action Programme* (forthcoming) – see www.dfes.gov.uk/sen

Department of Health, *National Service Framework for Children* (forthcoming).

Self-evaluation checklist

Assessments and reviews

How do you ensure early identification and effective intervention at School Action and School Action Plus?

Is the LEA meeting the six-month target for statutory assessment? ■

Are parents and children involved appropriately in assessments and reviews? ■

> *Are children as well as parents actively involved and encouraged to participate in assessments and reviews?* ■

> *Do you know why certain parents or children tend not to participate?* ■

> *Do staff use plain English and explain any technical terms, both in spoken and written communication with parents and children about SEN issues?* ■

> *Are people who do not have English as a first language offered interpreters for meetings and translations of key paperwork and letters about their child?* ■

Provision of services and equipment to meet assessed need

How quickly are services and equipment provided, following an assessment?

> *Are there any areas of particular difficulty or delay?*

> *What steps are being taken to deal with these?*

Are all children able to attend a *local* school, either mainstream or special? ■

Which groups of children have to travel out of area, or attend residential school, because their needs cannot be met locally?

How far can children and young people fully participate in the life of their school, and reach their potential?

Are pupil outcomes monitored?

What are the barriers to inclusion and how does the accessibility strategy/plan address these?

If there are placement difficulties for children with certain types of need, what steps are being taken to ensure that children have the option of staying with their families and having their educational needs met?

Skills and attitudes

Which teaching and learning support staff have been trained in disability awareness and core skills for working with children with SEN?

Are there any important gaps?

Is there a pool of staff trained in particular specialisms, that could be shared across schools?

If not, how are specialist skills developed and maintained?

What steps are taken to promote disability awareness among pupils?

Recruitment and retention

Is there a strategy to deal with recruitment and retention of key staff for children with SEN (for example, LSAs) who are employed by the school, or the LEA?

Is joint workforce planning undertaken with other agencies to help tackle staff issues (such as turnover, shortages, skills)? ■

4.2 Play, leisure and sport

This section will be of interest to:
✓ play and youth workers/managers ✓ leisure services staff ✓ holiday scheme organisers ✓ park managers.

See also: transport, supporting families.

Children and young people talking

I think disabled people should be taking part more in sports. They've done wheelchair rugby and you can tackle by touching. Like field sports like wheelchair cricket and golf they should do more like that... We do rounders...

Run by bullies...might as well be at home [Mainstream youth clubs].

Parents talking

The lady who runs that [scheme] is absolutely marvellous. I put Tracey in the special needs playscheme the first year and she didn't enjoy it at all. So we had a word and she said 'Oh I'll put her in the other one' and she thoroughly enjoys it.

Oh you can come and join our trampoline group, 'yeah bring him along' and you know perfectly well he's not going to be able to join in with a group because a) they won't know how to deal with him and b) they won't have the staff to deal with him. It's this thing about inclusion – people are very keen to be seen to be doing inclusion doesn't just mean saying 'Yes come along'.

It's too hard for me to take her [swimming now], there are no changing facilities at the pool where they run the class. I had to change Claire on a table outside where everyone else was sat. ... she's now 12 and it's not right.

Siblings

Going out is special for disabled families. For example, if my brother is sick we can't go out and my Mum doesn't get any sleep.

Findings

We asked disabled children and their families about their leisure time. They mentioned a range of mainstream and specialist services, including play groups, after-school clubs, youth clubs, holiday schemes, leisure centres and parks.

Like other children and young people, disabled children and their families really valued leisure activities, holidays and time with friends. However, they found it much more difficult to enjoy the same opportunities, because often services did not meet their needs. It was a struggle for families first to find out what was available, then to find something suitable to meet a child's specific needs and finally to meet any age and eligibility criteria. Families' accounts reflected the national shortage of inclusive and specialist provision, in the public, voluntary and private sectors. For families in greatest need, social services sometimes tried to make up for the shortfall by funding places on particular schemes, or providing a support worker, befriender or link worker. But resources were very limited.

These service gaps, which deny disabled children and young people basic play and social opportunities, also put extra pressure on family life, because parents miss out on the usual breaks from caring, and create a greater need for already thinly stretched social care services. Siblings in our research said they too missed out on play and leisure activities, and wanted to be able to do more things with their disabled brother or sister, but also to have an opportunity to do things without him or her, to be free from caring responsibilities.

After-school, play and holiday schemes

We found that where disabled children and their families could access appropriate leisure-time services they were very appreciative. However, the following issues were frequently reported as creating difficulties for families:

- shortage of suitable schemes, both mainstream and specialist, in all sectors;

- poor or fragmented information about local schemes;

- schemes claiming to be inclusive, but in reality only meeting some special needs;

- little or no local provision for some sorts of needs (such as autism), and gaps in services for different age groups;

- exclusion of children due to: lifting and handling policies; lack of provision for intimate care or medical needs; poor accessibility to buildings; lack of suitable toilet or changing facilities;

- siblings often having to attend separate schemes; and

- unhelpful attitudes from some staff, and reported bullying of disabled children and young people in many mainstream services.

In the context of scarce provision, families reported that often there was little choice or flexibility to meet an individual child's needs, which could result in inappropriate or unsafe placements. And because of short-term funding arrangements for many services, a scheme that had been found for a child one year could not be relied upon to continue the following year. There was also a view that some families were getting a lot more services than others, because they were more knowledgeable about services.

Youth

We found that disabled young people often wanted the opportunity to mix with their non-disabled peers out of school. But many also found it important to have a disabled peer group of friends to talk with and go out with, especially if they were in mainstream school. It was also important to young people to be able to go out independently from family.

Services working towards inclusion

Our research found that many statutory services were planning to make their mainstream services much more accessible to disabled children and their families, primarily in response to the requirements of the Disability Discrimination Act 1995. Audits of buildings and training needs were taking place in many services, and arrangements being made for all staff to receive appropriate training.

Features of good play, youth and leisure services for disabled children

Mainstream services working effectively towards inclusion are aware that significant cultural and practical change will be required. Whereas in the past disability was viewed as a minority concern, now effective managerial support and appropriate training is planned and provided for all staff. Performance management systems to support inclusion build positive attitudes, skills and behaviours into personal targets and competencies, as well as into departmental and organisational objectives, and reward achievement of these.

Services are made more accessible by extending the scope of:

- building adaptations;

- toilets suitable for disabled people;

- changing rooms (suitable for an adult and larger child/young person of different sex – baby changing facilities are not suitable for older children who need changing);

- wheelchair friendly paving and access gates (for example, to parks); and

- playground equipment suitable for children with mobility problems.

In designing inclusive services there is active learning from existing successful projects. Voluntary sector organisations can often provide helpful models. Staff from these may be approached as development workers, and to train staff. Disabled trainers are employed where possible, and disabled service users and their advocates are fully involved in the process of making mainstream services fully accessible. Specialist consultancies may also be used to consult with and plan services for this client group.

To ensure that all age groups and types of need are catered for, in a sector where there are multiple providers, there is a strategic approach to service planning. Multi-agency planning forums can be an effective mechanism for achieving this. Services which are effective at meeting disabled children's needs ensure that parents and children are represented on these forums, and may consider setting up a sub-committee or linked forum looking exclusively at provision for this special group.

At the same time as making mainstream services more accessible and inclusive, a certain level of specialist services is maintained, because it will take time for new services to become fully inclusive for all children. We know from our research that even specialist services or those who attempt to be inclusive often find themselves still excluding a significant proportion of children with specific needs (for example, medical, behavioural or intimate care), because of lack of skills or capacity. Truly inclusive services work towards including all disabled children, not only those who are easier to deal with. The case study overleaf illustrates a model that could be applied across a wide range of services.

The Individual Playcare Plan records only a child's support needs for this service: medical or SEN 'labelling' is avoided.

The model has been influential in the development of local joint commissioning of disabled children's services, and the recent attainment of Children's Pathfinder Trust status, where the aim is to move from a 'respite' service to a 'rights-based' service.

Critical success factors

- Leadership, through a dedicated post to oversee the work.

- Clear framework for providers.

- Pooled funding.

- Partnership with disabled children and their parents, and all relevant agencies.

- Staff paid to attend training and implementation meetings.

For further information, please contact:

Jacqueline Winstanley
Tel: 01204 334 119
Email: Jacqueline.Winstanley@bolton.gov.uk

Signposting

Children's Play Information Service and Children's Play Council – National Children's Bureau, 8 Wakley Street, London, EC1V 7QE. Tel: 020 7483 6000

Kidsactive: a national charity promoting play for disabled children, www.kidsactive.org.uk

ODPM, *Accessible Play Space Guide*, (forthcoming 2003).

Council for Disabled Children, *Dignity and Risk* (2003 forthcoming guidance including lifting and handling policies and practice).

Ask Us, 2002, CD Rom – a multimedia presentation of disabled children and young people's research into local public services. Available from: The Children's Society - www.the-childrens-society.org.uk/bookshop.

P Murray, *Hello! Are You Listening? Disabled Teenagers' Experience of Access to Inclusive Leisure*, York Publishing Services, 2002.

N Finch et al, *Disability Survey 2000: Survey of Young People with a Disability and Sport*, Sport England, 2001.

Self-evaluation checklist

To what extent are mainstream play and leisure services accessible to disabled children and their families?

What proportion of disabled children make use of local mainstream play, leisure and youth provision?

Are there any specific groups of children who tend to be excluded? (such as children who need medical care or help with toileting)?

How far do these families have to travel to access provision?

Are there any age gaps in service provision (eg between end of play and start of youth services)?

What steps are being taken to make services more comprehensive and inclusive?

Do all local swimming pools and sports facilities have:

wheelchair access (to buildings and facilities)? ☐

family changing rooms (that older children and opposite sex parent can use)? ☐

swimming and sports equipment to allow inclusion of disabled children? ☐

specialist and inclusive classes offering activities valued by users? ☐

Are parks accessible to disabled children and their families, in terms of:

access gates? ■

paths? ■

play equipment and swings? ■

toilets and changing facilities? ■

Is there a strategic approach to provision across services in statutory and voluntary sectors? (for example, planning forum, including disabled children sub-committee or forum). ■

Have there been recent evaluations of play, leisure and parks from the perspective of disabled children and their families, involving consultation with users themselves? ■

What were the key findings and actions?

_____

Have they been implemented? ■

Do all managers and frontline staff in mainstream services understand how services can enable disabled children to reach their full potential? ■

Do they have the skills and attitudes required to make sure that disabled users have full access to services and facilities? ■

4.3 Supporting families

This section will be of interest to:
✓ social workers ✓ managers
of family support services
✓ short-break care staff in
statutory and voluntary sectors.

*See also: skills knowledge and
attitudes, recruitment and
retention, user consultation and
involvement, joined-up services,
moving into adulthood.*

Children and young people talking

*It's a fine line, you need to give parents a break, but then you
need to consider the children, which is the difficult part about it.*

*I like people who can tell stories...not when they sit there and
drink tea, they go shopping and read books and knit.*

*The new ones [care staff] should ask their boss how disabled
children are. For example, if you can't move, they got to know if
you can't.*

Parents talking

*Brilliant...she was sensible, understood where I was coming
from, and tried to do as much as she possibly could.*

*Consistency is crucial and getting a few right people instead of
constant changes, which is very unsettling for all of us in the
family.*

*It's not only the fact that there isn't a lot of help out there, it's
also that... we have turned some people down, because they
were not suitable.*

*We said basically that they were making us and Leo do these
overnight stays or he couldn't have any respite, there wasn't any
alternative... So they took the complaint up and looked into it,
and agreed that in fact we were right and that they were trying
to make the child fit the service, rather than making the service
fit the child.*

Siblings talking

*Some friends don't understand why I can't come into town or
why I have to babysit but close friends, they understand.*

Findings

Families of disabled children have greater social support needs than other families. This is partly because of the barriers to services, such as nursery, play and after-school clubs, that give other parents a break from caring. But also because they are much less likely to receive informal types of childcare. Parents, as well as their disabled children, have fewer opportunities to see friends and pursue interests outside the home, and are often find it extremely difficult to arrange family holidays. Siblings may have restrictions in their leisure activities too, with greater caring responsibilities, and loss of parental attention. Research shows that families with disabled children are also more likely to live in poverty.

Statutory and voluntary support services in a locality may include:

- sitting services and home carers (for day or night);

- day, overnight or weekend fostering;

- residential and non-residential short-break schemes;

- social workers;

- domestic help;

- hospices;

- psychology and behaviour support services;

- counselling;

- support and self-help groups (for parents, disabled young people and siblings);

- advocacy (for parents and/or young people); and

- befriending schemes.

Overall picture of family support services

Where services were working well – and care staff were skilled and well-matched to the family – there was enormous gratitude. But our research with families overwhelmingly indicated that the most usual experience was a continual struggle to obtain consistent, reliable services to meet needs. Some families acknowledged the resource constraints that service managers had to deal with, but many of them also felt that more could be done to improve services.

Demand outstripped supply in all family support services, with tight eligibility criteria, and long waits for assessment and service provision, particularly in the statutory sector. Families who received services felt that they were too thinly stretched – saying they needed more support and more breaks from caring. It was not unusual to find that a family had to wait six months to a year for a care worker, and the same again if the carer had to be replaced. There were also concerns about equity, with many parents under the impression that those who 'shouted loudest' had the best services. And to find emergency cover – for a funeral or a parent going into hospital at short notice – was almost impossible.

There was a reliance on historic patterns of provision in the statutory sector, which often resulted in a lack of choice for families. For example, in many areas there was a strong emphasis on residential short-break schemes, with little or no opportunity to have home-based services, which many children and families said they would have preferred, and could have allowed resources to be used more effectively. Families also wanted greater flexibility over the type of domestic help offered and choice of carer.

Many issues were raised about the quality and reliability of care offered by both statutory and voluntary sectors (which were often funded by the public sector). Principally:

- frequent turnover of staff and lack of relationship building with child and family;

- missed appointments and failure to follow through with agreed actions;

- carers lacking basic skills in caring for disabled children, or not being briefed; and

- capability of carers to deal safely with medical needs.

Our research also confirmed the existence of service gaps, in particular:

- counselling, psychology and behaviour support services;

- services for children with specific needs (such as autism, technology dependent, lifting and handling); and

- culturally appropriate services *[see also section 1.5]*.

But, in the same area, there could be some excellent services for a particular group of children (for example, children with life limiting conditions).

When there were service gaps or other problems (for example, disputes between agencies about funding of care), parents had to go from one agency to another on their own initiative. A lack of accessible sources of information about services, local support groups and benefits, was a recurring problem for families.

Families in our research wanted a regular carer who had:

- good, age-appropriate, communication skills;

- disability awareness and respect for all members of the family;

- specific practical skills and experience in caring for disabled children (for example, administering medication, dealing with medical emergencies, using communication aids); and

- cultural sensitivity.

Families also wanted carers to be reliable and to work with other professionals to ensure that they understood a child's particular needs. The most basic request was for staff to ensure that they had read the child's file before coming to the home.

Many families wanted one person to whom they could turn for information, to advocate for them independently, and to get services to talk to each other. Formal keyworking schemes were highly rated by users, where these were in place. Case studies of keyworking schemes are given in sections 1.3 and 3.1.

User experiences of residential short-break schemes varied. Children and young people valued carers who:

- were 'good fun';

- respected them; and

- played or talked with them in an age-appropriate way;

and enjoyed residential short-break experiences where:

- they were grouped with other children of a similar age and abilities;

- they had choices about what activities they did or what food they ate; and

- they could take part in fun or exciting activities of the kind that their non-disabled peers would enjoy.

They were unhappy where:

- staff ignored them;

- they were in an ill-matched group and could not communicate or play with the other children (for example, a child with only physical disabilities being put in a group with children all of whom have learning disabilities, or who have different means of communication);

- where their medical or personal care needs were not properly met;

- where they felt unsafe because of other children's behaviour; and

- when their activities were more limited than those their non-disabled peers would enjoy.

Features of good family support services

Effective services give children and their families a genuine voice in their own assessments and reviews and in service design more broadly. They offer a range of options for meeting their needs, including community and home-based services, and a well-supported direct payments scheme for both parent carers and young people.

Regular carers are allocated to familes, who have the knowledge, skills and attitudes to deliver high quality, reliable services. Further information about staffing issues can be found in sections 2.1 and 2.2, which are cross-sectoral, and contain case studies relating to social care. Residential short-break schemes, and other group activities, are designed to meet children and young people's needs, by ensuring that children are grouped with appropriate age peers and offer a choice of attractive activities. Disabled young people themselves are actively involved in service development.

Up-to-date, comprehensive information about availability and eligibility for family support, and other services and benefits, is made available through a range of measures, for example:

- well-publicised, printed directories and web material – covering different providers and services – and available in different formats/community languages;

- one-stop shop for disabled children's services;

- keyworkers and frontline staff who are supported to provide a wide range of relevant information, and make links with other agencies; and

- children's information service (CIS).

A strategic approach is taken to planning and delivering family support services, for example, through a cross-sectoral multi-agency forum *[see section 1.3]*, or a forum bringing together all the social care providers in an area, statutory and voluntary. The principles of needs-based planning are used to map, analyse and reconfigure services *[see sections 1.1 and 1.2]*. For family support services this means gathering and analysing information about:

- needs and preferences of disabled children and families in the area, through direct user consultation, including minority ethnic groups;

- staffing resources and skills across agencies;

- existing and available funding sources for different agencies;

- current service configuration, including gaps and overlaps;

- opportunities for joint working; and

- lifting and handling policies, intimate care policies and other related policies and working practices that can lead to exclusion.

With this understanding, services identify key priorities for change and develop multi-agency initiatives, such as joint training or keyworking, using pooled budgets. The multi-agency forum may also be used to put together a transitional funding package, to move the balance of services from buildings-based short-break schemes to home-based or short term fostering services, while building up a suitably trained and committed pool of community-based carers that families can rely on.

The National Service Framework for Children is to set standards for disabled children's services across a range of agencies, in particular social services, health and education.

Transitional arrangements for young people moving from children's to adult services are covered in section 3.3. Issues relating to long term residential care did not fall within the remit of this study, but references are given in the Signposting section.

Good practice

Nottinghamshire County Short Breaks Service

In 2000 Nottinghamshire created an expanded county-wide team to provide short breaks for disabled children and young people, bringing together the resources and specialist skills of smaller teams located in different parts of the county. The aim was to provide high-quality, flexible and safe care for children who are 'permanently and substantially' disabled, covering: autistic spectrum disorder, physical and learning disabilities, and chronic health conditions. The service currently has 130-135 carers providing a service to over 170 children.

The services offered are:

- day and overnight fostering, in the foster carer's home;

- befriending, to help children to access community facilities;

- sitting service within the child's home; and

- overnight care within a child's home (under development).

Foster carers, befrienders and sitters, are recruited and supported by a professional short-break care team of 6.5 FTE social workers, a social work assistant, paediatric nurse, occupational therapist (appointment pending) and administrative support. Professional staff have complementary skills and experience relevant to working with disabled children, including specialisms in autism, fostering and children's medical needs. The team was designed to be able to respond quickly to children's needs, rather than relying on professionals from other teams/agencies.

There is an explicit policy emphasis on providing safe care. Around 75 per cent of the carers have prior experience and/or qualifications relevant to working with disabled children. Short-break foster carers are assessed using the NFCA competency-based model and are approved via the agency's fostering panel. Befrienders and sitters also have a thorough assessment and are approved through a separate panel established by the agency for this purpose. Full criminal record checks are carried out on all potential carers along with health, personal and employer references. Prior to application there is an obligatory seven session induction course.

There is also a care protocol, which is applied for all children where there is a specific healthcare need or condition requiring management (such as epilepsy). All carers then receive child specific training and a written safe caring document is produced and signed jointly by the parents/carer, the paediatric nurse and the child's consultant (where appropriate). The occupational therapist will help to train carers in the safe handling of children with physical disabilities, and the provision of equipment, and will contribute to risk assessments.

The most recent survey of users (2001) indicated high levels of satisfaction among service users (children and their primary carers). However, demand outstrips supply for this high-quality service. A contract carer scheme is being developed using Choice Protects money for those on the waiting list. Ongoing attempts are also being made to recruit more carers, targeting those already working in disability services.

Critical success factors

- Optimised skill sharing through creation of larger, multi-disciplinary team;

- High-quality staff recruitment and training; and

- Professionally managed care protocol.

For further information, please contact:

David Robinson – Team manager
Tel: 01623 629741

 # Signposting

Sharing Value Directory: Information about services which disabled children and their carers particularly commended, www.sharingvalue.co.uk

Triangle *Two-Way Street* Training video and handbook for professionals about communicating with disabled children and young people. Available from: Triangle (tel: 01273 413141; www.triangle-services.co.uk; email: info@triangle-services.co.uk).

Department of Health, *A Parents's Guide to Direct Payments*, Department of Health, 2003.

Department of Health, *National Service Framework for Children* (forthcoming).

J Morris, *Still Missing? Vol 1: The Experiences of Disabled Children and Young People Living away from their families*, The Who Cares? Trust, 1998.

J Morris, *Still Missing? Vol 2: Disabled Children and the Children Act*, The Who Cares? Trust, 1998.

For other useful publications about user experiences of family support services see:

Joseph Rowntree Foundation: www.jrf.org.uk/knowledge/findings

Norah Fry Research Centre (University of Bristol): www.bris.ac.uk/Depts/NorahFry

The Social Policy Research Unit (University of York): www.york.ac.uk/inst/spru

Self-evaluation checklist

Has there been a recent multi-agency assessment of family support needs and services in the locality, involving disabled children and their parents? ▪

Or is one planned? ▪

Did or will this review include a radical challenge of existing patterns of services – for example, the balance of homecare and residential short-break services, the availability of behaviour support and counselling services, and so on? ▪

What shortfalls or gaps in services were indicated? (For example, services for children of different ages, with different types of impairment, with different cultural backgrounds and first languages other than English, support groups for disabled children/parents/siblings?)

_____

How will any shortfalls be remedied?

_____

Has there been any attempt to rationalise and maximise resources across agencies? ▪

What lead times are families experiencing for services?

time from initial contact with service to initial assessment

_____

time from initial to full assessment (if applicable)

_____

time from final assessment to provision of a service

_____

time to provide another regular worker should someone leave

_____

response time/capability of providing cover in emergency situations (such as family funeral)

_____

Do services plan ahead and provide cover for staff sickness and holidays? ■

Has there been a recent review of the quality of staff involvement in both home-based and residential short-break care settings? ■

Were families (including children) asked to evaluate this? ■

What were the findings, and has follow-up action been taken?

Do assessments include full and respectful involvement of children and families? ■

Are different service options offered? ■

What happens if there is a conflict between a child and an adult's wishes?

What arrangements are there to secure adequate child protection, both in residential and home settings?

Is a direct payments scheme in operation, both for parents and young people? ■

What is the level of take-up?

Has it been effectively advertised? ■

What support is available to help families to operate the scheme, including vetting of workers to help avoid child abuse?

What feedback has been obtained from users and what actions have been taken as a result?

What are the lifting and handling policies of different agencies?

How do service managers ensure that families are not excluded on account of these?

How do families find out about the available family support services in an area (from statutory and voluntary sectors) and their eligibility for them?

Is there is a single point of contact? ■

How are these services advertised?

Is information available in community languages? ■

What arrangements, if any, are there in place to help families to access services and benefits, beyond strictly social care services? (For example, play, leisure, youth, sport, housing and benefits.)

Are care workers supported to offer this? ■

Is there a keyworking system to help families to obtain care that is co-ordinated between agencies? ■

If not, what arrangements are in place to ensure that agencies work together effectively?

Are joint funding protocols (such as pooled budgets) in place, for example, between social services and health for home-based care that includes medical and social care elements? ■

Are services working towards implementation of the National Service Framework for Children? ■

4.4 Equipment

This section will be of interest to:
✓ social workers ✓ occupational therapists ✓ physiotherapists
✓ home care services ✓ orthotics and prosthetic services ✓ community equipment services ✓ audiology services ✓ education services
✓ wheelchair services.

See also: housing, planning services to meet needs.

Young people talking

I pushed myself around all day, crying my eyes out, and was so tired that I could no longer move my arms [using replacement manual wheelchair when electric one broken down].

Families talking

You would think, well he needs it, give it to him. But it's not like that, you have to really bang your head to get something.

If he needed a new manual wheelchair, it might be months before it appears on the scene. That's where his physio is very good, because she sees when he's near needing it and she will get the ball rolling so when he does actually need it, we've got it. But we are very fortunate, we have a very good physio.

The toilet seat became too small. It took eight months to get a new one.

You go to other parts of the country and you see kids in wheelchairs and they've got all these nice sprung seats and that and you think 'Well where did you get them from then?'

Like this chair here. He's had it since he was three. She the occupational therapist made a case for it. Ordinarily they're not available for children under five...It helps us all, every minute of every day almost because it means he can sit with us.

Findings

Equipment services include:

- orthotics (for example, footwear and supports);

- prosthetics (artificial limbs);

- wheelchair services;

- community equipment services (including home nursing aids and minor adaptations);

- communication aids; and

- educational aids.

Throughout our study, our findings have emphasised the importance of services that are based on an understanding of users' needs. The families we spoke to identified a number of problems mainly associated with slow provision of equipment or a service that was not responsive to need. For example, the time taken for equipment to arrive could mean that children outgrew it before it was ready. This meant that parents and professionals constantly had to anticipate needs and ask for equipment in advance, in the hope of getting it by the time it became necessary.

As with other services, parents felt they had to be demanding and determined to get their child's needs met. They sometimes commented that when they finally got the equipment, they were pleased with what was available and the benefits it gave to their child, but still felt that they had been put through an unnecessarily long and complex process to get it. Parents also noticed that they sometimes had to develop more expertise about the specific equipment that their child needed than the professionals who were meant to be advising them. Long waits for equipment also have implications for the health of other family members as well as the child – for example, parents may suffer back problems from lifting and moving a child without a hoist.

Families were frustrated when there were delays in the provision of comparatively cheap pieces of equipment, which could make a big difference to a child and family's quality of life. When difficulties were due to inadequate funds, they were aware of inconsistencies in what was available from region to region, and according to the time in the financial year. Sometimes families experienced additional delays, because of having to wait for a new budget year. Further frustrations arose from dealing with more than one agency at a time, or users themselves having to get a proportion of funding from charitable sources. Inflexibility in the service provided also caused problems – for example, where children were only allowed to use education equipment at school, when they could clearly have benefitted from using it at home as well, or where they were not allowed to take equipment with them when they changed schools.

Poor-quality equipment and slow, inefficient repairs services, can leave service users facing inequality and poor clinical outcomes. Poor services can also infringe human rights – for example, if children are denied communication aids that are essential to allow them to speak and express themselves.

Major changes in equipment services, particularly community equipment services, have been put in place, largely in response to Audit Commission studies. These have highlighted concerns about:

- planning of services, which have often been provided on the basis of local custom and practice, rather than from an assessment of current or future needs;

- efficiency and value for money of equipment services;

- eligibility criteria being unclear for both users and staff; and

- lack of clinical leadership and senior management involvement in many services.

The recent developments include:

- Community equipment services (CES) traditionally provided by both health and social care must be fully integrated by 1 April 2004: including pooled funding, a single store, and a single point of contact.

- All integrated CES will be required to introduce a single assessment process and shorter timescales for both completion of assessments and for delivery of equipment.

- Guidelines for commissioning CES have been produced jointly by the Audit Commission and the DH Integrated Community Equipment Services (ICES) Implementation Team.

Wheelchair services in England are currently being reviewed by the Modernisation Agency. A Wheelchair Services Collaborative will test and implement changes in the approach to service delivery throughout 2003. In Wales, the Specialised Health Services Commission for Wales has undertaken a complete review of wheelchair services and is implementing agreed changes. Additionally the Audit Commission has published guidelines for commissioning wheelchair services.

Orthotic and prosthetic services have been slower to remedy their problems with delays and long waiting times. However, recently the Audit Commission has also produced separate commissioning guidelines for these services.

Features of a good service

Sometimes the correct equipment can transform the quality of life of a disabled child, and make caring for the child much easier for the family. Developing technology means that at its best, equipment can be highly sophisticated. On the other hand, simple equipment, such as chairs and toilet seats, can be very helpful at minimal cost.

Agencies delivering effective equipment services:

- carry out regular reviews of policy, strategy and operational delivery;

- establish standards and targets to improve the quality of services;

- consult and involve service users sensitively;

- measure and quantify unmet need;

- promote inclusion and independence;

- invest in equipment to avoid higher spending elsewhere; and

- train and support staff.

In many areas equipment services are targeted mainly at older people. Good services are tailored to children's specific needs and demonstrate awareness of the:

- acceptability of the equipment – in terms of how it looks and feels – children do not want equipment that they think is ugly or outdated;

- need for equipment to be provided promptly, and replaced or adapted, as they grow;

- role of correct equipment early in a child's life to help alleviate or prevent further physical problems;

- importance of mobility equipment in allowing children to access education, play and social facilities which are crucial to their development; and

- central role of communication equipment in children's personal and educational development, both in and out of school.

Good practice

Auditing equipment for children across health, education and social services in Trafford

Paediatric occupational therapists and physiotherapists in Trafford assess needs and recommend equipment for children across health, education and social services. A large amount of equipment is now located in schools, homes and a central store. It has become clear that accurate information is needed about:

- where equipment is;

- when and whether it can be reallocated;

- how it is being maintained; and

- what its life expectancy is.

A Paediatric Technical Instructor post was created with health funding to collate and itemise equipment, and log children's details on a database. The postholder also:

- gathers user guidelines from equipment suppliers;

- develops systems for therapist assessments;

- develops systems for allocation, maintenance and repair of equipment; and

- develops policies and procedures for providing equipment and processing orders.

The technical instructor has responsibility for maintaining the database and monitoring equipment provision for therapy services across different providers. This helps ensure that users receive a co-ordinated and efficient service.

Critical success factors:

- one person has responsibility for monitoring equipment across a range of different services. This helps ensure that service users get a co-ordinated service and maintains accountability for the overall quality of service.

- up-to-date information is maintained about the location and use of all equipment, allowing it to be tracked, serviced, checked and reallocated to best meet children's needs.

For further information, please contact:

Paula Moore
Joint Head of Service
0161 283 4617/9

Signposting

Audit Commission, *Fully Equipped*, Audit Commission, 2000.

Audit Commission, *Fully Equipped 2002: Assisting Independence*, Audit Commission, 2002

Commissioning Guidelines for wheelchair, orthotic and prosthetic services – www.audit-commission.gov.uk

Department of Health, *Guide to Integrating Community Equipment Services*, Department of Health, 2001

Commissioning Guidelines for Community Equipment Services – www.icesdoh.org

B Beresford, *Community Equipment: Use and Needs of Disabled Children and their Families*, Social Policy Research Unit, University of York, 2003.

J Ford, *Speak for Yourself*, SCOPE, 2000. A report about disabled people's experiences of communication aids services.

Council for Disabled Children, *Dignity and Risk*, (2003 forthcoming guidance including lifting and handling policies and practice).

Department of Health, *National Service Framework for Children* (forthcoming).

Whizz Kidz – a national children's charity to give disabled children and young people independent mobility. www.whizz-kidz.org.uk

Peggy and Friends – a charity that provides information, advice and practical support to parents and carers of limbless children. www.peggyandfriends.org

Self-evaluation checklist

Are equipment services planned and commissioned to meet measured needs? ▪

Are services planned according to service users' needs? ▪

Are future needs projected? ▪

Does equipment meet clinical need? ▪

Is there clinical leadership? ▪

Are contractors subject to quality standards? ▪

Is their performance monitored? ▪

Are the Audit Commission's guidelines on commissioning services being followed? ▪

Are services working towards implementation of the National Service Framework for Children? ▪

Are children consulted on their views of services and equipment? ▪

Are parents and families consulted? ▪

How often is equipment rejected or unused?

Are young people and parents represented on local community equipment services management boards? ▪

Are users' views and experiences taken into account in designing services? ▪

Are children's specific needs accommodated by providing child-friendly waiting areas and staff? ▪

Are staff who carry out assessments trained to work with disabled children? ▪

Are measures taken to provide equipment that is acceptable to children? ■

Is assessment child and family centred? ■

Are single assessments in place where possible? ■

Are community equipment services integrated? ■

Will community equipment services meet 1st April 2004 target for integration? ■

Have pooled budgets been established? ■

Are stores being integrated to promote a quick response to users' needs? ■

Are enough funds allocated to meet identified needs? ■

Are funds intended for disability equipment being spent on these services? ■

Are eligibility criteria set appropriately to meet need? ■

Are staff informed about the support available from voluntary organisations? ■

Do they share this information with families? ■

After a child's needs have been assessed, how long does it take for a piece of equipment to arrive? ■

Does this meet national and local targets? ■

Are users satisfied with waiting times? ■

Do repairs meet target times? ■

Are they carried out to an acceptable standard? ■

Is equipment that is no longer needed re-issued to new users promptly? ☐

Is equipment tracked and recycled? ☐

Are services accessible to minority ethnic families? ☐

Are assessments sensitive to users' cultural and language needs? ☐

Is there a complaints process? ☐

Is information about it made available to all service users? ☐

4.5 Transport

This section will be of interest to:
✓ Local Education Authorities (LEAs) ✓ schools ✓ social services ✓ hospital transport services ✓ transport planners ✓ transport co-ordinators.

See also: moving into adulthood, skills knowledge and attitudes, play, leisure and sport.

Children talking

I don't like travelling on the bus because it's boring...talking gets boring. [long journeys]

It stinks...ciggy smell. [taxi used by school]

Parents talking

I know they do have those low-floor buses but round here it's touch and go whether you get one, or if there is one, then there's already a buggy on there. The Saturday before, we didn't get home until eight o'clock in the evening because I waited two hours for a bus.

Some of the drivers are difficult and others are lovely.

And she [taxi driver] wound down the window and said 'Can you hurry up. I've got other children to collect' and I said 'I'll take him to school myself if that's your attitude. You obviously can't deal with special needs kids.' She phoned me up on my mobile and gave me a lot of grief.

Taxis can be a nightmare – you can't pre-book a disabled one. You have to hope that the wheelchair will fit in the back of the cab. That could be improved really.

I think the thinking behind it [no eligibility for mobility allowance until the child is three] is that a child under three isn't properly mobile so you would have to have a pushchair or you would have your own transport. But they don't take into account the extra problems...

Findings

The Audit Commission report *Going Places* concluded that local authorities had done much to provide good home-to-school and social services transport, but that there were opportunities to improve the services further and increase the focus on the needs of service users.

In our study, disabled children and their parents talked about transport services as a key factor in their access to other services and a social life. Transport is a particular issue for disabled children because:

- home-to-school journeys are often longer for children who attend special schools;

- children with limited mobility may need transport even where journeys are short;

- disabled children may have regular hospital appointments for which they need transport; and

- families with disabled children are more likely than others to be socially disadvantaged and not have access to a car.

The families we spoke to commented mainly on home-to-school transport. LEAs have a duty to provide or arrange free transport to and from school for certain pupils, including those with special educational needs. Transport to school may be provided in buses, or by taxis. Escorts are sometimes provided. For some families in our study, experiences were good, with friendly, helpful and reliable staff that children liked and trusted. Some parents commented that they were only able to go out to work because of the transport provided to take their children to and from school. However, where things went wrong, parents were often very uneasy with putting their child into the hands of people they disliked or distrusted.

Entitlement to help was sometimes an issue. For example, where families had chosen a mainstream school other than the nearest, because they felt that this was more suitable for their children's needs, some were not given any help with transport because this was only provided for the school nearest to home. For some parents, this meant struggling with loading heavy wheelchairs and children in their own cars – one mother was starting to have back trouble as a result. On the other hand, there were comments from some young people about difficulties of lengthy journeys on local authority transport to and from school or college, which could take up to an hour and a half.

Other issues included:

- For older children, the freedom to travel was important for developing an independent life and social experiences. Some felt that they were restricted by difficulties in using public transport, and expressed a preference for being able to get out and about on their own, rather than being dependent on help from their parents and friends.

- Some parents, particularly mothers, commented on the improved accessibility of public transport, for example, buses providing space for wheelchairs. However, they would not always know in advance whether the bus would be accessible or not. Some felt that travelling by public transport was not an option.

- Motability schemes can provide families with suitable vehicles for their own use. However, some of the families participating in our study had found that the scheme was inflexible and could lead to unexpected and distressing extra charges, for example, for repairing minor scratches and damage, or for excess mileage costs.

Transport was an important issue for most of the families in our research. Help such as mobility allowance, bus passes, accessible public transport, school and hospital transport and Motability vehicles were all valued. However, existing services sometimes lacked sufficient flexibility to meet families' needs.

Features of a good service

- Core service quality standards are set, and contracts or service level agreements encourage service providers to meet these standards. Route planning, funding, and the use of service providers are regularly reviewed to identify ways of improving standards.

- Eligibility criteria for assisted travel (for example, free school transport, bus passes) are reviewed and monitored to check they are meeting needs.

- Transport provision for disabled children is part of broader transport and planning policy, with implications for environmental and social inclusion policy. Partnership working arrangements can include:

  - partnership with other statutory bodies (for example, health);

  - joint planning arrangements with neighbouring authorities;

  - working with local passenger transport executives; and

  - working with the voluntary sector.

- Staff have the right skills to assess children's transport needs, and review these at least every 12 months.

- Equipment and vehicles are suitable for the needs of the children who are using them. They are in good repair and are maintained in a safe condition.

- Escorts and passenger assistants are used by local authorities to help to improve safety for children, and prevent bullying on journeys to school. This increases parents' confidence in the service and avoids them having to drive their children everywhere themselves. Training is carried out with drivers and passenger assistants, and security checks made.

- Local authorities regularly consult disabled children and young people, and their families, about the transport services they use.

- An accessible and clearly explained complaints service is in place.

- Consultation and complaint outcomes are used to review quality standards to ensure that service users' views are being heard and acted upon.

Good practice

Getting There! Training for young people using public transport in Hull

The City of Hull has used funding from the DfES Pathfinder Initiative to produce a teaching pack called *Getting There!* The pack aims to promote independent travel on public transport for 14-19 year old students with special educational needs (SEN).

Getting There! is the first project to take the approach of identifying and developing the skills that young people with special educational needs require to be able to travel on their own, for example, to pursue further education or training. The project is based on an imaginative story, which presents students with the day-to-day practicalities and problems of travelling. Using a mixture of group discussion, tasks and role play, seven modules cover essential skills, such as journey planning, handling money, safety and communication skills.

The initiative has been successfully piloted over seven months in Hull, and has now been launched locally, with further conferences to promote the pack in London, Birmingham and Sheffield.

Getting There! received a great deal of interest from other LEAs when showcased at a recent DfES transport conference. The cost of transport for students with disabilities is often very high, and training for independent travel can save LEAs money in the longer term. In recognition, Hull was awarded funding for the production of teachers' packs, CDs and three conferences to promote the project to a wider audience.

Critical success factors:

- Consultation with Connexions, schools, colleges and social services which had identified lack of access to independent travel as a key obstacle to SEN students taking up further education and employment.

- Approach which builds the confidence and skills of the students and allows them to practise these in a safe environment.

- Active promotion of the pack by Hull LEA, with planned delivery, assessment and transition planning.

For further information, please contact:

Rayma Crawford, Education Officer (Client Services)
Tel: 01482 613162
Email: rayma.crawford@hullcc.gov.uk

 ## Signposting

Audit Commission, *Going Places*, Audit Commission, 2001.

Audit Commission, *Improving Home to School Transport for Children with Special Educational Needs: A Practical Handbook for Managers*, Audit Commission, 2001.

Department for Education and Skills, *Home to School Transport for Children with Special Educational Needs – Good Practice Guidance*, Department for Education and Skills, 2001.

Self-evaluation checklist

Is eligibility for home-to-school transport meeting the needs of disabled children? ☐

Is there clear local guidance about eligibility that is regularly reviewed? ☐

Is this guidance being followed? ☐

Is eligibility considered as part of SEN assessment, and reviewed annually? ☐

Do decisions comply with the SEN code of practice? ☐

Is school transport for disabled children safe? ☐

Are needs for equipment assessed and reviewed by trained staff at least every 12 months? ☐

Is equipment for transporting disabled pupils available when needed? ☐

Is it well maintained? ☐

Are staff trained in using equipment? ☐

Are the vehicles used matched to children's needs? ☐

Are escorts/passenger assistants provided to meet children's health and safety needs? ☐

Are staff trained to deal with children becoming unwell while travelling? ☐

Are procedures in place for identifying if children or parents are not present, at either pick-up or drop-off points? ☐

Are security checks carried out on all staff? ☐

Does school transport meet quality standards for disabled children? ☐

Have standards been set in consultation with disabled children and their families? ☐

Do children arrive on time for school? ☐

Are journey times reasonable and are travelling conditions comfortable for children? ■

Are families and children consulted about transport services? ■

Are regular consultations carried out with service users? ■

Are services reviewed in the light of consultation outcomes? ■

Is there a complaints system and have service users been informed about it? ■

Are complaints monitored and acted upon? ■

Are local transport services responsive to the needs of disabled children and their families? ■

Do local public transport services provide disabled access? ■

Do local transport plans include provision for disabled people? ■

Has local public transport route planning taken account of the need for accessibility of local services via public and assisted transport? ■

Have the needs of disabled young people (aged 16-19 years) both considered, in terms of access to further education, employment and social opportunities? ■

Are partnership working arrangements in place for transport services provision? ■

Are local authorities, health services, passenger transport executives and neighbouring authorities involved in partnership working arrangements? ■

Is access to public transport for disabled children and their families taken into account in planning services? ■

Is the accessibility of local services for disabled children and their families included in the local transport plan? ■

4 Inclusion in everyday life

4.6 Housin

This section will be
✓ housing officers ✓
workers ✓ occupationa
therapists.

*See also: equipment, joined-u
services.*

Young people talking

The new bathroom makes life really easy, I can just drive-through, like when I come home from school.

Families talking

We were desperate for the work to be done because every time he wanted to go to the toilet he had to crawl upstairs so I didn't like that.

Our dream is that we would have an en suite bedroom for her where she would have everything arranged and suitable for her use. Sometimes she will say 'Sorry Mummy I need the toilet', and this makes me feel really bad. 'Why do you have to feel sorry? We all have to have to go the toilet,' and she says 'Yes but I know you are really tired.'

The occupational therapist comes out to say what Carrie needs and they tell us what is suitable and what building we can and cannot do, and then you get the forms filled in, and then you've got to get the architect, you've got to get the builder. That's just things that you don't need. When you've got a child with special needs, you've got to do all this, you've got to sort it out.

The council were very keen for us to have the bare minimum and the basic stuff which would have meant that in another five or six years we would have been asking for more work to be done.

...e families we spoke to in our study described
...suitable housing or adaptations. This included
...s, private tenants and council tenants. In
particular they mentioned needing:

- more space, particularly where a disabled child needed room for equipment;

- a downstairs or ensuite bathroom or toilet;

- single level accommodation, downstairs bedroom, or lift;

- soundproofing or separate rooms, particularly for siblings; and

- disability adaptations (special baths, taps, doorways, and so on).

The main source of help with housing adaptations depends on the type of property. For owner occupiers, the main way is through applying for a Disabled Facilities Grant (DFG), which provides means-tested payments of up to £25,000, or more if local authorities consider it necessary. For people in social housing, the housing authority may undertake adaptations themselves, apply for a DFG, or rehouse the family in more appropriate accommodation. An initial assessment of the family's needs is carried out by a social services occupational therapist (OT), followed by an assessment by the housing department of the home and the likely cost of adaptations. Social services departments may also provide funds for needs not met by the DFG.

While we found some support had been provided to families seeking to adapt homes or find new accommodation, they had experienced a number of barriers and frustrations, and inconsistencies in what was made available and to whom. Sometimes the process of assessment, choosing adaptations and having work done took so long that the child outgrew the adaptations before they were complete. While the occupational therapist's expertise in recommending adaptations was welcomed by families, many also felt that they would like more expert advice on what is available, and on how to choose architects and builders who are experienced in the type of work they need.

Difficulties with the DFG were frequently described. Some families in our study had noticed inconsistencies in who was entitled to what help. This was sometimes to do with low paid employment, leaving families worse off in terms of grants and benefits than if they were unemployed. It also related to different funds and services being available in different regions, and inconsistencies in decisions arising from variations in annual budgets. Even when they were entitled to help, many families told us that they were expected to contribute a quantity of money that they simply could not afford. As a result, adaptations were sometimes not carried out at all.

At times rehousing appeared to be the best option. However, where families had been moved to new areas, this had sometimes created problems with their access to services and could mean losing the support of other family members. Also, deciding to move to a new home meant that existing plans for adaptations were cancelled, often leaving the family in inappropriate accommodation for longer.

Features of a good housing service

Suitable housing is a central need for many families with disabled children. Well-planned and properly adapted homes make caring for a disabled child much easier. Children have more independence and privacy, and a better quality of life. Suitable adaptations and equipment also help to protect other family members from injuries related to lifting and moving the child.

Successful housing services for families with disabled children take an approach that is founded on a thorough understanding of needs. For example, at the assessment stage, the needs of the entire family are taken into account, such as siblings needing separate rooms or soundproofing to allow them privacy and quiet uninterrupted sleep. Cultural needs are also taken into account, such as providing space for prayer where appropriate. Interpretation and translation services are provided where needed, keeping families fully informed throughout, and making sure that their views are heard.

Needs-based assessment takes account of longer-term as well as immediate needs, and ensures that work is carried out within an appropriate timescale. If adaptations are to be carried out, families receive support in managing the building process and architects. Where adapting the existing home is not practical, information about options is offered, and professionals help to match families with the most appropriate housing, whether in the social housing or the private sector.

While adaptations or moving home can be expensive, it is sometimes more cost-effective for public funds to be used to help families improve their housing rather than spend money on long-term help from care staff, or more state benefits because parents, for example, have been incapacitated by back problems. Housing participation in multi-agency forums could allow agencies to consider the balance of resources across different services and their implications.

Services can also seek to maximise their use of resources, and help meet families' housing needs, by offering advice and support in claiming benefits and grants, and where appropriate linking families to other sources of funding, for example, the Family Fund or other voluntary organisations.

Good practice

Bradford Disabled Persons Housing Service

Bradford DPHS went live as a citywide service in April 2002 – the first local authority-based DPHS to be set up. It provides a specialist housing service for adults, young people and children with disabilities or health needs, regardless of income, or tenure. In February 2003, Bradford's housing stock transferred to Bradford Community Housing Trust (BCHT – a new RSL). The Bradford DPHS now operates through BCHT.

Bradford provides a 24-hour internet-based lettings system called Homehunter, a local government award winner in 2003. Disabled people and families can access housing either by searching Homehunter themselves, or, if their needs are for more specialised property or adaptations, the DPHS will try to acquire the stock on their behalf. It maintains close links with housing associations to develop bespoke accommodation for clients, such as one-off new builds, property conversions or 'state of the art' extra care schemes.

Since the stock transfer, the DPHS now manages the adaptations budget for BCHT. The unification of rehousing services for disabled clients in need and the reletting of existing adapted properties has led to savings of around £600,000 on major adaptations costs in a 12 month period.

The service includes:

* a fully networked adapted property database of over 2000 social rented properties, listing all adaptations carried out;

- a mechanism for all empty adapted properties to be let to disabled clients;

- a Disability Housing Register of all clients in need;

- first point of contact for hospital discharge cases; and

- occupational therapy input to assess clients and void properties so there are no undue delays.

Properties are advertised on the internet so clients can locate and view them from their own homes or at PC kiosks installed at accessible public locations across the city. For those who are not on line, staff can take laptops out on home visits to show or search for available stock

In future the DPHS is considering:

- viability of delivering a removal assistance scheme to help clients relocate; and

- delivering a comparable service to owner occupiers, in particular to help address the needs of the black and minority ethnic population in Bradford.

Critical success factors

- simplifying and streamlining the rehousing process, to make it more transparent and approachable for service users;

- involvement of families in specifying their needs;

- high level of cultural sensitivity with respect to housing needs; and

- better matching of clients with suitable housing.

For further information, please contact:

Atis Krumins, BCHT Housing Access & Advice, DPHS, 3rd Floor, Central House, Bradford, BD1 1DJ
Tel: 01274-432323
Email: atis.krumins@bchtgroup.org
Web: www.bradfordhomehunter.co.uk

Inclusion in everyday life

4.6 Housing

Signposting

HoDis – The National Disabled Person's Housing Service, 17 Priory Street, York, YO1 6ET, www.hodis.org.uk

Joseph Rowntree Foundation: Findings of Completed Research Projects on Housing Services for Disabled Children and Their Families. www.jrf.org.uk/knowledge/findings

Good practice examples: Sharing Value website www.sharingvalue.co.uk

B Beresford and C Oldman, *Housing Matters: National Evidence Relating to Disabled Children and their Housing*, The Policy Press, 2002.

M Bevan, *Housing and Disabled Children: The Art of the Possible*, The Policy Press, 2000.

V Shaw, *Needs First: A Good Practice Guide for RSLs to Prioritise Tenants' Needs for Adaptations*, HoDis, 2002.

F Heywood, *Money Well Spent: The Effectiveness and Value of Housing Adaptations*, The Policy Press, 2001

B Beresford and C Oldman, *Making Homes Fit for Children: Working Together to Promote Change in the Lives of Disabled Children*, The Policy Press, 2000.

4 Inclusion in everyday life

Self-evaluation checklist

Are families fully informed about housing options? ▪

Do families have a single point of access to information about their housing needs, how to claim grants and benefits, and how to go about commissioning work? ▪

Do they have an advocate or contact to support them through the whole process? ▪

Are all staff working with disabled children and their families aware of housing needs and benefit entitlements for this group, or able to refer them to the right place for further information? ▪

Have families been consulted about the effectiveness of information services and how they might be improved? ▪

Are the housing needs of disabled children and their families properly assessed? ▪

Do social care assessments (or other relevant multi-disciplinary assessments) of disabled children include housing needs? ▪

Do assessments of housing needs demonstrate awareness of the whole range of different disabilities and support needs disabled children may have? ▪

Are assessments culturally sensitive? ▪

Is the assessment child and family centred – are all family members consulted? ▪

Do assessments of the suitability of housing include considerations of the locality, community, family support and access to services? ▪

Are families being matched to appropriate housing? ▪

Is support provided for those looking in the private and owner occupier sectors? ▪

Are families informed of all options, including moving and having their current home adapted? ▪

Are tenants offered support in becoming owner occupiers? ▪

Do families feel that they have genuine choices?

Are longer-term needs as well as immediate ones taken into account?

Are families receiving a good-quality service?

How long does it take for adaptations to be carried out once the need has been assessed?

How often does the family turn down the options offered because they cannot afford their contribution to the cost? Are they given support in finding alternatives?

Are families with disabled children, and minority ethnic families, inclined to be in poorer quality or more overcrowded accommodation? What steps are being taken to address this?

Do local agencies have effective joint working arrangements in place?

Has there been a recent multi-agency review of housing, that considered the needs of disabled children?

Have its recommendations been implemented?

Do local agencies have a shared awareness of the housing needs of families with disabled children?

Do housing strategies specify the needs of families with disabled children?

Are families consulted about housing services and strategies?

Are services working towards the implementation of any standards set out in the National Service Framework for Children?

5

Appendices

5 **Appendices**

Appendix I: Acknowledgements

We would like to thank all those who have contributed to this study. In particular we are grateful to: the children, young people and their families who gave their time to speak to us; Triangle, our user reference group; and the service providers from our five main study sites and good practice examples.

The project was managed by Karen Naya and Denise Davies, under the direction of Morag MacSween. Other members of the project team were David Browning, Beverley Fitzsimons, Edana Minghella, Louise Gitter, Heather Harper and Sonia McKenzie.

The user research was carried out by the Thomas Coram Research Unit.

Appendix II: Parent and carer factsheets